SEPTEMBER 11ᵀᴴ FAMILIES FOR PEACEFUL TOMORROWS

TURNING OUR GRIEF INTO ACTION FOR PEACE

by David Potorti
with Peaceful Tomorrows

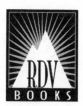

Published by RDV Books/Akashic Books
©2003 The Tides Center/Peaceful Tomorrows

ISBN: 0-9719206-4-8
Library of Congress Card Number: 2003106947
All rights reserved
First printing
Printed in Canada

Cover design by Keith Campbell
Layout by Sohrab Habibion and Alexis Fleisig

Grateful acknowledgment is made for the permission to print the following photographs and video stills: front cover photo of view from the stage at the April 20, 2002 march on Washington ©Peaceful Tomorrows; back cover photo of Rita Lasar with the Japanese HANWA delegation outside St. Paul's Church in New York City ©David Potorti; back cover photo of David Potorti, Ryan Amundson, and Colleen Kelly claiming their rights in Washington Square Park, December 2002 ©Peaceful Tomorrows; photo on p. 22 ©Jenny Warburg; photo on p.25 ©Jenny Warburg; video still on p.38 ©Voices in the Wilderness; video still on p.42 ©Voices in the Wilderness; photo on p.43 ©David Potorti; photo on p.45 ©David Potorti; photo on p.46 ©Jenny Warburg; photo on p.48 ©Peaceful Tomorrows; photo on p.63 ©Eva Rupp; photo on p.65 ©Kelly Campbell; photo on p.76 ©Kelly Campbell; photo on p.81 ©Peaceful Tomorrows; photo on p.96 ©Kelly Campbell; photo on p.97 ©Kelly Campbell; photo on p.102 ©Barry Amundson; photo on p.103 ©Jenny Warburg; photo on p.106 ©Peaceful Tomorrows; photo on p.120 ©Kelly Campbell; photo on p.127 ©Natalie Behring; photo on p.139 ©Peaceful Tomorrows; photo on p.149 ©Kelly Campbell; photo on p.155 ©Peaceful Tomorrows; photo on p.156 ©Ellen Shub; photo on p.164 ©Peaceful Tomorrows; photo on p.170 ©Derrill Bodley; photo at bottom of p.185 ©Jenny Warburg; photo on p.188 ©Linda Wan; photo on p.190 ©David Potorti; photo on p.195 ©Linda Panetta/Linda@soawne.org; photo on p.196 ©Linda Panetta/Linda@soawne.org; photo on p.198 ©AP/Hussein Malla; photo on p.217 ©Peaceful Tomorrows; photo on p.218 ©Peaceful Tomorrows; photo at top of p.221 ©David Potorti; photo at bottom of p.221 ©Barry Amundson; photo on p.222 ©David Potorti; photo on p.223 ©Andrew Rice; photo on p.225 ©Peaceful Tomorrows; photo on p.229 ©Ward Morrison/wardpix.com; photo on p.231 ©Ward Morrison/wardpix.com; photo on p.244 ©Jenny Warburg.

Grateful acknowledgment is also made for the permission to reprint the lyrics to the songs "Each to Give" on p.95–96 ©Derrill Bodley; and "The Art of Being Kind" on p.97 ©Kristina Olsen, inspired by the Ella Wheeler Wilcox poem by the same name that comprises the song's first verse.

RDV Books
130 Fifth Avenue, 7th Floor
New York, NY 10011

Akashic Books
PO Box 1456
New York, NY 10009
Akashic7@aol.com
www.akashicbooks.com

Introduction

As we opened our eyes on the morning of September 11, 2001, few of us realized how many goodbyes that day would bring: to people we loved and places we knew, to our plans for the future and our sense of control over our lives, to the trust we had in our safety and our nation's institutions. We had no idea how many holes would open up on that day, not just in the terrain of lower Manhattan, or Washington, or Shanksville, but in our hearts and in our spirits. Into those holes went not only the memories of thousands of individuals, but thousands of expressions of love they would have brought into the world.

Those of us who lost family members that morning found ourselves in particularly painful positions. Our losses were not simple murders, but international incidents, symbols, and public events. Billions of people experienced the exact moment of our loved ones' deaths. And whether we liked it or not, their deaths would become public property. They would be invoked on any number of occasions, for any number of purposes, by people we didn't know, and in many cases, didn't agree with or care for.

Most of us chose to turn off our televisions and radios as we dealt with our difficult grief. But some of us, recognizing the public nature of our losses, chose to redeem them by making public statements that frequently were at odds with conventional wisdom about what families of the victims must be feeling. It was through those statements that the people who formed September 11th Families for Peaceful Tomorrows met and organized themselves into a nonprofit group seeking alternatives to war and working to end the cycle of violence.

We had no business knowing each other. We were different ages, came from different places, and had decidedly different backgrounds, personalities, and life experiences. We weren't saints by any stretch of the imagination, and had frequent disagreements about what we were doing. We had a lot to learn about the world and about each other.

But like disparate people who get stuck together in a doorway during a thunderstorm, we came to realize that human beings pass their days in endless combinations, have more in common than they think, and can work together toward just about any shared goal. Honoring our lost family members has always been that goal, and it is our memories of them that constantly keep us on track in what we choose to do—or not to do—as members of Peaceful Tomorrows.

While September 11 remains for many the genesis of new fears, new suspicions, and a redoubling of efforts to secure themselves and their possessions, for us it was a day that demolished the belief that we could ever be truly independent of each other. It was a day when the walls came down, not up. It was a day when we realized that our weapons could no longer protect us. And that our children would never be safe unless unseen children on the other side of the world were safe as well.

One can look at our public witness—speaking at schools, places of worship, rallies, and conventions in twenty-nine states and eight foreign countries—and ask how it could possibly replace the people we lost that day, or ever set the world straight again. In fact, we have been the biggest beneficiaries of our own work, and have derived from it a sense of personal peace, security, and focus. We refuse to believe in an us-versus-them world, recognizing instead that we can, and must, create the world we want to live in. It is an ongoing process. No one will do it for us.

The deaths of our family members stand not as a legacy of hatred and fear but as a challenge to aspire to better things.

September 11 remains as an invitation for Americans to enter the new millennium and to join the rest of the world, accepting the challenge to deal honestly with the global responsibilities that come with being a global superpower.

This book tells the story of how members of September 11th Families for Peaceful Tomorrows recognized and rose to those responsibilities; how speaking out connected us with each other; how people around the country and the world extended their hands in friendship to our group; and how we continue to fill the holes in our hearts with new connections, new love, and new possibilities.

From our shared experiences, I've written a running history of our group, including my own participation. Along the way, you'll find personal essays written by a number of our most active members. And I've included some of the e-mails from around the world that have been posted to our website's guestbook, giving a taste of the issues raised—and emotions aroused—by our work. These e-mails, along with press releases, links to media coverage, newsletters, and ways to join or contribute to our organization, can be found at www.peacefultomorrows.org.

In the days following September 11, America had a unique opportunity to transform the deaths of our family members into the birth of a new paradigm for the planet, an arrangement that recognized our mutual humanity, mutual needs, and mutual goals. The hand of friendship that was offered to us by the people of virtually every nation on earth remains extended. We continue to reach out our hands in return, and in so doing, hope that our nation will collectively do the same.

David Potorti
Cary, North Carolina
July 2003

We must overturn so many idols,
the idol of self first of all,
so that we can be humble,
and only from our humility
can we learn to be redeemers,
can learn to work together
in a way the world really needs.
—Oscar Romero, *The Violence of Love*

Chapter One

September 11, 2001, 8:46 A.M. A week after Labor Day, summer shows no intention of leaving North Carolina. As birds chirp in a thick canopy of trees, the still air hanging outside of David Potorti's bedroom window is already warm enough to eliminate the possibility of eating lunch outdoors. He opens one eye and fixes it on his bedside clock. A first-time father in his forties, he spent a good part of the night rocking his 14-month-old son to sleep, earning him the privilege of sleeping in—one of the good things about downsizing his life as a writer in Los Angeles for a life in the 'burbs. His wife, a college English teacher, works away from home only two days a week, leaving both of them plenty of time for family. He rolls over and sees her peeking through the bedroom door with their son: Daddy's up! The pair climbs into bed with him for a group hug. It is, he decides, an exquisite little moment.

It is the last one he will experience for a while.

Because at that exact hour, in lower Manhattan, his oldest brother, Jim, is getting hit by an airplane: American Airlines Flight 11, the first plane to crash into the World Trade Center. A few minutes later, as Potorti stands in his backyard drinking a cup of coffee, the phone rings. His mom says, *"I'm very concerned about the kamikaze attack."* Kamikaze attack? *"On the World Trade Center."* The World Trade Center? And then, to drive the point home, *"Your brother works there."*

His wife turns on the television and he sees the images—the burning tower, the second plane, and the fireball—that will come to run like a film loop in his head. His brother works on the 95th floor of the North Tower. He knows it's 110 stories tall.

And as he estimates the point of impact by counting down floors from the top, he realizes that the gaping hole and billowing smoke are coming from exactly where his brother should have been sitting, and his stomach turns. Is he there at this hour? Is he on a stairwell, screaming in the middle of chaotic evacuation? Potorti continues to watch—and as he sees the first, and then the second tower collapse, he wonders: Am I watching my brother die, right now, on live television?

* * *

In New York City, the skies are postcard blue: It is an absolutely gorgeous day. Rita Lasar, a widow in her seventies, rises in the rent-controlled Lower East Side high-rise she shared with her late husband, Ted, and pops a cigarette into her mouth. They raised two sons here, running a small electronics business around the corner, and one winter day Ted sat down on the recliner chair that still sits in her living room, and didn't get up. But she still lives here, and has a life befitting a woman of her stature, a life of plays and museums and books and old friends.

As is her fashion, she starts her day at the kitchen table in her nightgown, with a cup of coffee—the strong kind, from San Francisco—and listens to WBAI-FM, the listener-supported Pacifica Network radio station. That's when she hears it: A plane has hit the World Trade Center, only two miles from where she's sitting. She rushes into her den, flips on the ancient portable TV, and sees black smoke pouring out of the North Tower. Still wearing her slippers, she hustles down the hallway to her friend's apartment at the other end of the building, the one with a southwest view encompassing the Twin Towers.

Together they step out onto the balcony, where the TV image she's just seen is playing out in real time against the crystal blue sky. They arrive just in time to see the second plane hit the second tower. At that moment, she realizes that whatever is happening is not an accident.

And at that same moment, she realizes that her kid brother, Abe, is working in one of those burning buildings.

* * *

A world away in the North Bronx, Colleen Kelly has the distinct feeling it's going to be a great day. Kindergarten started the week before, and her daughter cried every morning on her way to school. But on September 11, her daughter isn't crying. And for this mother of three young kids, that's a victory worth savoring. A nurse practitioner, she lives with her social-worker husband, Dan Jones, and their two boys in a former residence for Catholic priests, a gabled three-story house that stands like a relic amid the brick apartment buildings that surround it.

Kelly works at a high school health clinic about two blocks from where she drops off her daughter. She's on the phone with Sister Suzanne, a nurse in East Harlem, when the nun says, "Did you hear about the plane hitting the World Trade Center?" The clock on Kelly's desk reads 9:23 A.M. She turns on the radio—where the news is still frantic and confusing—and asks her co-workers if they know that something serious is going on downtown. She gets a sick feeling in her stomach, the same feeling she gets whenever she flies, because she's deathly afraid of getting on airplanes.

Kelly spends the morning fielding calls from her mother and two sisters, who are concerned about her brother Billy. She reassures them that Billy works at Park Avenue and 59th Street—miles away from the chaos. She returns to her radio to hear a live report from a Brooklyn rooftop: The reporter starts screaming in mid-sentence that one of the towers is collapsing. Kelly is overwhelmed with compassion for the people there. Her high school, an enormous urban institution with 4,200 students, begins to make plans for counseling kids who might be touched in some way by the loss of life downtown.

At 11:15 A.M., Kelly's phone rings. It's her sister Mimi, and she's got bad news: Billy was at the World Trade Center for a breakfast conference. Kelly starts screaming, "No!" She screams it over and over again. The nightmare she's been listening to has just become her own.

* * *

In Hartville, Missouri, September 11 is shaping up to be a care-free day for Ryan Amundson. A University of Missouri grad with a degree in sociology, he woke up early—which was not typical for the 24-year-old—to start his first day as a substitute teacher at his old school, a gig he's taken while waiting for his Peace Corps nomination to go through. He's living with his parents, and his mom is kidding around, snapping his photo like it's little Ryan's first day of school.

He's teaching his first class—which as a substitute teacher is more like steering Jell-O—and when he walks down the hall to make some copies, he notices that television sets are on in every classroom. He asks himself if this is what kids do in school all day, and when he jokes with the school superintendent, he picks up on a pervasively somber mood. As he walks back to his class-room, he encounters teachers congregating in the hall, who tell him that both towers of the World Trade Center have been hit by airplanes, as well as the Pentagon, where his older brother, Craig, works.

Standing in front of a television, he takes in the images of smoke and flame in Washington. It's such a small hole, he decides, in such a huge building, one with thousands of workers. What are the odds that Craig could have been in the line of fire?

He calls his dad at work and learns that nobody's heard anything. They're beside themselves with worry, but they think Craig is probably fine.

Ryan tries to pick up the hopeful vibe. But as far as the carnage he's witnessed on television, he concludes that this is the beginning of World War III. And he's horrified.

* * *

It's 9:30 A.M. in Washington, DC, and Eva Rupp, a program analyst with the National Oceanic and Atmospheric Association, can't get on the Internet. She picks up the phone, and that's not working either. She looks up from her desk and notices that, oddly, no one seems to be around. An emotional co-worker comes down the hall with the news that a plane has accidentally hit one of the Towers in New York. Rupp wonders how in the world a pilot could make a mistake like that, until others come with the news that it wasn't a mistake.

Everyone gets scared—after all, they work in a thirteen-story, well-marked federal building in Washington—but it isn't until ten minutes later, when they hear that the Pentagon has been hit, that they really panic. Still, no one's supposed to leave the building until the order comes to evacuate. Five minutes later, Rupp takes off, deciding it isn't worth waiting on protocol, not when it feels like the country is being attacked.

She tries to call her mom in Stockton, California, but all the phones are dead. There are helicopters over the city as she makes her way home to downtown Washington, and she hears rumors that twenty-two other planes are unaccounted for. F-16 fighter jets scream over the city and she thinks they're going to intercept them. She wonders: Who's next? Why has this started? Is this ever going to end?

By noon, she gets through to her mom and learns the bad

news: Her stepsister, Deora Bodley, might have been on United Flight 93, which crashed at 10:10 A.M. near Shanksville.

The F-16s she heard had been headed for Pennsylvania.

* * *

In the Oakland, California duplex shared by Barry Amundson, Craig's brother, and partner Kelly Campbell, September 11 has yet to begin, leaving them to enjoy their first good night of sleep in days. They were in Chicago the past weekend for Campbell's brother's wedding, and after celebrating, flying home, and heading into work on Monday morning, they hadn't had so much as a minute to catch their breaths.

The phone rings at 7:15 A.M., and Craig's mom is crying: Planes are flying into buildings and one of them has hit the Pentagon. Campbell hands the phone to Amundson, pulls their little TV out of the corner, and plugs it in. They watch as the North Tower collapses. The coverage switches to the Pentagon, and numbness sets in as Barry tries to connect what he's seeing on the tiny screen with real life. They see where the damage is, and after visiting Craig's office the year before, they know it's on the other side of the building. But his office had moved since then—where would he have been sitting?

Barry and Kelly call in to work—a San Francisco ad agency and an environmental nonprofit—to tell them they won't be in till afternoon, till they get word that Craig is all right. He called his family after the World Trade Center was hit, but he hasn't called since.

They learn a lot of people are staying home from work that day. Nobody wants to take the BART trains, which go under San Francisco Bay. And all those helicopters flying over the city are making people nervous.

* * *

In White Plains, New York, a suburb just north of the city, Phyllis Rodriguez is taking advantage of the splendid weather to initiate a new exercise regime. An artist and teacher of homebound children, she imagined her walk would get her home by 9 A.M., but when she arrives at 9:20, the doorman tells her that one of the Twin Towers is on fire. Rodriguez runs up the stairs to her fourth-floor apartment, turns on the TV, and hits the button on her answering machine, where messages are waiting. There's one from her son, Greg, who works on the South Tower's 103rd floor. *"There's been a disaster at the Trade Center, but I'm okay,"* he reports. *"Call Elizabeth"*—his wife.

As Rodriguez listens to the message with one eye on the television, she sees a replay of the second plane hitting the South Tower. She calls everyone in the family, and they all ask her the same question: Where was Greg when he made the phone call?

"He must have called from outside the building," Rodriguez replies. "Who would have called from a burning building?"

Chapter Two

For the family members who would later form Peaceful Tomorrows, the ensuing days and weeks were remarkably similar. As September 11 gave way to September 12, 13, and 14, it became clear that their loved ones would not turn up in burn units, be found walking the streets with amnesia, or emerge from the rubble of the World Trade Center or the Pentagon. The Rodriguez's would lose their 31-year-old son, Greg, who worked for a technology subdivision of Cantor Fitzgerald in the South Tower. Lasar would lose her 55-year-old brother, Abe Zelmanowitz, on the 27th floor of the North Tower, where he worked for Blue Cross/ Blue Shield. Colleen Kelly would lose her 30-year-old brother, Billy, a marketing executive at Bloomberg LLP, who happened to be at a breakfast meeting at Windows on the World and otherwise had no reason to be at the World Trade Center. Potorti would lose his 52-year-old brother, Jim, a vice president at Marsh & McLennan, on the 95th floor of the North Tower. Barry and Ryan Amundson's brother, Craig, 28, would perish at the Pentagon, where he was a multimedia illustrator for the Army. Derrill Bodley would lose his daughter, Deora, age 20, after she had taken a seat on flight 93, which left an hour earlier than the plane for which she was ticketed. Their losses would be multiplied a thousand times over, each one the loss of an entire world.

As smouldering flames still consumed the fallen towers, blanketing New York with a smell compared by Rita Lasar to "a pot handle burning on the stove," the Bush Administration identified Osama bin Laden—a figure well-known to the U.S. government but a cipher to most Americans—as the perpetrator, and

Afghanistan—resonating, if at all, as the site of a Soviet invasion in the 1980s—as his "host nation."

It quickly became clear that the United States would be bombing Afghanistan, sooner rather than later. And if the Administration earned accolades for its restraint—waiting weeks, rather than days or hours, to begin—the reality that it would lead to civilian death was undeniable, and deeply troubling, to the family members. They had seen, firsthand, innocent toddlers traumatized by the loss of a parent. They had witnessed elderly parents weeping for their grown children. They had seen brothers and sisters just like them—confident, coming into their own, certain of their futures—reduced to nothingness. To be touched so closely by violence and death was, for them, to demand an end to the possibility that others would suffer the same fate.

And because the killing was being undertaken in the names of their loved ones and their families, they felt something else: ownership. This war would be *their* war, fought in *their* names. This gave them the will to speak out. And it was by speaking out that they became known to their communities—and to each other. If September 11 united them in loss, it was the bombing of Afghanistan that united them in their desire to attain justice without killing more innocent people.

Phyllis and Orlando Rodriguez found themselves challenged, in a way most people rarely are, by their own beliefs. They opposed the death penalty. They were opposed to war. They supported human rights efforts. Orlando had taught sociology and criminology at Fordham University in the Bronx for twenty years.

"From the first day, even though my husband and I were in tremendous shock and grief and fear, we sensed that this criminal act was going to have political consequences," Phyllis said. "We were very afraid of a military reaction. We felt that even through that shock and grief, we couldn't sit by and not say any-

Missing person notices, New York City, September 2001

thing. We would instead use our position as grieving parents to draw attention to the fact that not everybody was going to go along with it, and we would try to stop it."

On September 14, they e-mailed a statement, entitled, "Not in Our Son's Name," to friends and relatives, who themselves circulated it on the Internet, where it quickly began turning up on websites around the world.

Not in Our Son's Name

Our son Greg is among the many missing from the World Trade Center attack. Since we first heard the news, we have shared moments of grief, comfort, hope, despair, fond memories with his wife, the two families, our friends and neighbors, his loving colleagues at Cantor Fitzgerald/ESpeed, and all the grieving families that daily meet at the Pierre Hotel.

We see our hurt and anger reflected among everybody we meet. We cannot pay attention to the daily flow of news about this disaster. But we read enough of the news to sense that our government is heading in the direction of violent revenge, with the prospect of sons, daughters, parents, friends in distant lands dying, suffering, and nursing further grievances against us. It is not the way to go. It will not avenge our son's death. Not in our son's name.

Our son died a victim of an inhuman ideology. Our actions

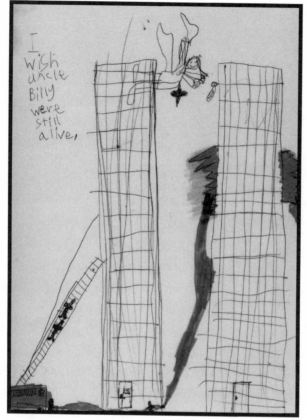

I wish uncle Billy were still alive,

Drawing by Dylan Jones, November 2001

should not serve the same purpose. Let us grieve. Let us reflect and pray. Let us think about a rational response that brings real peace and justice to our world. But let us not as a nation add to the inhumanity of our times.

> *Phyllis and Orlando Rodriguez*
> *September 14, 2001*

* * *

CNN's Maria Hinojosa, who would emerge as the only American television journalist consistently giving voice to alternative views on the war, saw the statement and interviewed the

Rodriguez's for a segment on the September 25 edition of the network's *Live at Daybreak*.

"You think at first that it's going to make you feel better to hit the kid who bullied your kid, but if you take a deep breath and think about it, you realize that it is not a productive way to react," Phyllis said. "When I hear talk, thoughtless talk, of 'showing them how strong we are,' I see people like my son, who just happened to be at the wrong place at the wrong time. I see people like my son dying in other lands, and that hurts me."

They were less conciliatory in a letter to President Bush, to whom they suggested, "It is not the first time that a person in your position has been given unlimited power and came to regret it." In an interview with the *New York Daily News* (September 19, 2001), Orlando said, "I know there is anger. I feel it myself. But I don't want my son used as a pawn to justify the killing of others. I'm not willing to give our government carte blanche to take away our freedoms in the name of public safety." For the Rodriguez's, touched so intimately by the tragedy, it was no time to mince words. It was time to honor their son by holding tight to their convictions.

> Dear President Bush:
>
> Our son is one of the victims of Tuesday's attack on the World Trade Center. We read about your response in the last few days and about the resolutions from both Houses, giving you undefined power to respond to the terror attacks.
>
> Your response to this attack does not make us feel better about our son's death. It makes us feel worse. It makes us feel that our government is using our son's memory as a justification to cause suffering for other sons and parents in other lands. It is not the first time that a person in your position has been given unlimited power and came to regret it.
>
> This is not the time for empty gestures to make us feel better. It is not the time to act like bullies. We urge you to think about

how our government can develop peaceful, rational solutions to terrorism, solutions that do not sink us to the inhuman level of terrorists.

Sincerely,
Phyllis and Orlando Rodriguez
September 17, 2001

* * *

Rita Lasar shared the horror, the uncertainty, and the compassion for all victims of the September 11 attacks that took her brother's life. In the days following the tragedies, she was adamant about keeping the blinds closed on her apartment window, the one with a view of the Empire State Building, out of an irrational fear that she would see an airplane fly into it.

But it was President Bush's speech at the National Cathedral on September 14 that would cause her to pull the blinds open

Fresh Kills Landfill, Staten Island

and rejoin the rest of the world. That Friday was the first time since the attack that Lasar's younger son, Raphael, had been able to reach her apartment, an easy journey from New Jersey suburbs now rendered virtually impossible by bridge and tunnel closings, subway shutdowns, and security checkpoints.

"I was scared to death that something would happen to a member of my family," Rita said. "So in the midst of the grief for the one who had died, there was this fear that more people were going to die, and I wanted to protect my children at all costs."

They wanted nothing of the television news—they just needed to be together. The President spoke while they were out to lunch. When they came back, a longtime friend of Raphael's from the neighborhood called them and wanted to come over. "Did you watch the President's speech?" he asked when he arrived. And then: "He mentioned your brother."

"It is said that adversity introduces us to ourselves," Bush observed during the speech. "This is true of a nation as well. In this trial, we have been reminded, and the world has seen, that our fellow Americans are generous and kind, resourceful and brave. We see our national character in rescuers working past exhaustion; in long lines of blood donors; in thousands of citizens who have asked to work and serve in any way possible. And we have seen our national character in eloquent acts of sacrifice. Inside the World Trade Center, one man who could have saved himself stayed until the end at the side of his quadriplegic friend . . ."

Lasar's kid brother, Abe Zelmanowitz, worked on the 27th floor of the North Tower and could have escaped easily—in fact, he called his brother and sister-in-law, who begged him to leave, in the midst of the crisis. But he decided to stay with his wheelchair-bound friend, Ed Beyea—a large man, too heavy to be carried—until the firefighters arrived. Had the building not collapsed, his strategy would have succeeded. Instead, his story became an anecdote that Lasar realized was being used as a call to war.

"I couldn't believe it was my brother that the President of the United States was talking about," Lasar says, acknowledging that it didn't mean much at first. "But the next thought I had was, my country is going to use my brother's heroism as justification to kill innocent people in a place far away from here. And that just made my brother's death worse—the idea that it was going to be a justification for somebody else dying." On September 17, she wrote a letter to the editor of the *New York Times*.

To the Editor:

My brother, Abe Zelmanowitz, was on the 27th floor of 1 World Trade Center when the first plane hit. Although he could have gotten out of the building, he chose instead to stay with his friend, a quadriplegic who could not get out. President Bush mentioned his heroism in his speech at the National Cathedral on Friday.

It is in my brother's name and mine that I pray that we, this country that has been so deeply hurt, not do something that will unleash forces we will not have the power to call back.

Rita Lasar
New York, September 17, 2001

Four days later, Lasar appeared as a guest on *Democracy Now in Exile*, the Pacifica Radio Network's flagship program hosted by Amy Goodman and broadcasting from a former firehouse a short walk from the Twin Towers site. The program had moved from local outlet WBAI-FM into "exile" as a result of a bitter battle among station management, listeners, and the Pacifica board, which threatened to undermine the historic commercial-free, listener-supported network. Lasar was an active supporter of the station, and knew Goodman from the struggle to keep it independent.

Now she found herself in the unexpected position of appearing on the show to talk about her brother's death. The night before, President Bush had made a speech to a joint session of Congress in which he threatened, "You are either with us, or with the terrorists." Lasar said she was "heartbroken" over the President's speech and Congress' lockstep reaction, and read her letter to the *Times*. Then she remembered her brother by reading a poem he had written about himself years earlier:

> I dreamed I died and went to heaven, and when I got there, they asked me what kind of person I had been, and I said, 'Not so good.' So they sent me down to hell, and when I got there, they asked me what kind of person I had been, and I said, 'Not so bad.' So they sent me back to earth.

"That was my kid brother," Lasar said. "Not so good, and not so bad. This country must allow itself to see its own reflection in the mirror of this horror. We cannot continue to think of ourselves as innocents abroad. What happened ten days ago was the delivery of this message."

* * *

David Potorti, who lost his oldest brother, Jim, at Marsh & McLennan's 95th floor offices in the North Tower, was driving from his sister-in-law's house in New Jersey to his parents' house in upstate New York when he heard the National Cathedral ceremony on his car radio. He found in the words of the Reverend Billy Graham, who also spoke that day, a militance that brought him enormous discomfort.

"Today we say to those who masterminded this cruel plot, and to those who carried it out, that the spirit of this nation will not be defeated by their twisted and diabolical schemes," Graham said. "Some day those responsible will be brought to justice, as President Bush and our Congress have so forcefully stated . . . We also know that God is going to give wisdom and courage and strength to the President and those around him. And this is going to be a day that we will remember as a day of victory."

Having spent a good part of the morning listening to talk radio hosts demanding that we bomb "them" (whoever they are) and "ask questions later," he had little patience for what he interpreted as Graham's invocation of the spirit as an invitation to war. "I felt like he was christening a battleship," Potorti said.

In the days that followed, he would contrast Graham's words with those of his parents, both churchgoing Catholics: His mother, who bent over in pain when she learned that her son was dead, said, "I don't want anyone else to feel the pain I'm feeling right now." His father, a Fourth Division Marine veteran of World War II, accepted the need for some kind of military response but had a far more somber view of the realities of war than the cheerleading media. A buddy from the service, who had earned a Purple Heart, would bring the family communion in the days after September 11. When the local paper asked for a quote, David said, "I think we should seek justice, but we should not punish other people to seek justice."

A print journalist and television marketing producer, Potorti had moved to North Carolina to earn a Masters degree in Folklore and to document music and labor history. In late September, an invitation to write an opinion piece arrived via e-mail from the editor of the *Philadelphia City Paper*. Potorti wrote "A Political World" on October 4, 2001, which expressed his hopes in the wake of his brother's death.

> I'm hopeful that we will hear more voices, more outlooks, and more options in the weeks to come. I'm hopeful that we will be civil with each other as we share them. And in the end, I'm hopeful that we will love our country enough to look at it, and what it does, honestly, critically, and productively. Unlike President Bush, I cannot speak for my brother, Jim. I cannot declare war in his name. I can only hope that we create a better world than the one he left on September 11.

But it was a written piece inspired by NPR commentator Cokie Roberts that exposed Potorti's views to a larger audience. Roberts's patrician dismissal of Congressional opponents of the Afghanistan war as "none that matter" made Potorti so angry that the wrote a reaction minutes after hearing her.

"It's a jaw-dropping statement when you think about it, one that says nothing and yet says everything," he wrote. "There was opposition to the bombing. But how much? From whom? But before you go demanding simple facts or objective reportage, let's cut to the chase: *It doesn't matter* . . . It's equally handy at explaining our current crisis. Are the militaristic responses to the terrorist attacks likely to endanger the lives of more American civilians? *None that matter.* Will the war on terrorism endanger the civil liberties of Americans at home? *None that matter.* Will bombing Afghanistan cause any significant improvements in the lot of the innocent Afghan people? *None that matter.*"

He pitched the piece to Alternet, an alternative Internet news service, and learned that it was being syndicated with the title, "I Lost My Brother on 9/11: Does He Matter?" The essay soon touched a nerve with far-flung readers on the web.

* * *

For Derrill Bodley, a music professor at the University of the Pacific in Stockton and Sacramento City College, the first opportunity to publicly address the death of his daughter, Deora, who had been studying to be a child psychologist, came on September 13. Concerned with backlash for the crimes, and the threat of racial violence, school officials held an impromptu gathering at a central quad that drew 18,000 students and a number of speakers, including Bodley.

"I said, 'This is not about lashing out, this is not about vengeance, this is not about retaliation, this is about justice, and justice is a complex issue,'" Bodley recalls. "I tried to give them some kind of a motivational speech, and at the end of it, I said, 'Let's roll'" (the words of Flight 93 passenger Todd Beamer, which were later copyrighted by his widow).

That same day, Bodley sat at his grand piano. He had written two hundred original songs, and they had all come together over time, "like jigsaw puzzles." But this time, a song just came out "all of a piece." The song was "Steps to Peace."

"It expressed my longing to know where my daughter was," Bodley said. "But at the same time, it was an answer, saying that there's no need to wallow in sorrow, there's no need to worry or to wonder. The answer that I heard when I finished, and I started crying, was, 'Don't worry, Dad, I'm all right, it's okay, just do the right thing.' There are things that people think of in terms of religious experiences, or spiritual experiences—that when people die, the spirit can speak or can be felt. And I can accept that. I want to, as far as my daughter is concerned."

At a White House reception for Flight 93 families on September 24—ostensibly to recognize their lost loved ones for sparing them a presumed second suicide crash in Washington—Bodley handed the President a copy of his *Steps to Peace* CD. After the families had moved down a receiving line, Bodley heard a Marine armed with a piano, playing "Strangers in the Night" and other inconsequential numbers. He finagled himself an opportunity to play Deora's song and explained its message to the crowd.

"People came up afterwards and said, 'It really helped a lot for you to do that,'" Bodley recounted. "And it certainly has been helpful for me to feel like it helps other people."

At his daughter's memorial service on September 21, which was Derrill's birthday, he told the *San Francisco Chronicle*, "We must not retaliate in kind as if our cause allows us to." Of the name of America's new mission, dubbed the day before as

"Operation Infinite Justice," he said it "frightens me more than the terrorist attacks. I shudder to think they chose it because they think God is on their side. That is what terrorists think."

* * *

The days following the death of Craig Amundson at the Pentagon were complicated by restrictions on air travel. For brother Barry and partner Kelly Campbell, it meant a grueling cross-country trip from San Francisco to Chicago to Baltimore to the Fort Belvoir military base in Virginia, at a time of endless flight cancellations. Ryan and his parents started driving from Missouri the night of September 11, and arrived the next day.

It became clear that while there were generational differences of opinion inside the families, Barry, Ryan, and Kelly were feeling the same way about the impending military action.

"It was a conversation that flowed naturally out of our grieving," said Barry Amundson, "and it struck me that although people in our family covered a spectrum of political beliefs, from 'progressive' to 'conservative,' we were able to have this conversation in our mourning for Craig. The kind of violence that came to my brother was something that we wished on no one else, and it dawned on me that we were experiencing the horror of war and violence, the same as others who were in the wrong place at the wrong time."

"So in the midst of all of this grieving, and going to briefings at the Pentagon and the Family Assistance Center, and heating up food and trying to take care of each other, we started talking about this feeling," Kelly Campbell said, "and about the need to do something." Because they were a military family, they also felt that their words might carry an extra weight in affecting public opinion.

Campbell was familiar with managing media campaigns

from her nonprofit work. Wary of having their words misrepresented, and remembering how disruptive and time-consuming a recent visit from a local television crew had been, they decided that a newspaper opinion piece was an ideal format for their message. A neighbor on the army base who did public relations work for civil rights groups fortuitously offered the use of her home office, with computers and a fax machine.

Barry and Kelly started calling and faxing newspaper editorial departments to see if there was any interest, and settled on the *Chicago Tribune:* mainstream, middle-American, well-read. It was a particularly poignant choice for Campbell, who had been in Chicago the weekend before the attacks for her brother's wedding. One of his wedding guests, an Indian, had been assaulted on a Chicago street in the days following September 11 because "he looked like a terrorist."

"I feel like it's a part of being human to be violent, but that it's also a part of our instinctual survival process to question the past and seek reconciliation when mourning," Barry Amundson said. "When grieving, we can experience a gamut of emotions, and all of them are valid. Anger is one of those emotions, but coming to rest on it is not healthy—that warning was made in the military's own pamphlets about bereavement. Unfortunately, I feel that in our society, we are taught that anger is the only valid response and that retribution and vengeance at whatever cost to others is glorified. It makes for an easy plot element in a feature-length film—or a simple way to discuss a tragic situation on the nightly news."

I am only one
But still I am one;
I cannot do everything,
But still I can do something;
And because I cannot do everything
I will not refuse to do the something I can do.
—Edward Everett Hale

Chapter Three

If local newspapers were the launching pad for the families' statements, it was the Internet that took them to a worldwide audience. The essays quickly made their way across the country, appearing on websites for local and national peace groups and churches, into people's personal web logs, and onto discussion groups. And they swiftly crossed the oceans to appear on sites in Japan, Germany, Britain, France, Australia, New Zealand, Bangladesh, Cuba, and beyond.

At the Chicago offices of Voices in the Wilderness, a group committed to ending the sanctions against the people of Iraq, it was the essay in their local paper that they noticed first, and the Internet that led them to others.

"We thought, well, this is incredible courage," recalls Voices founder Kathy Kelly, twice nominated for the Nobel Peace Prize. "These people are speaking from an extraordinary place of depth and passion. So we felt that even though normally we're focused on issues related to Iraq, we should step aside from that and try to give reverence to these words that were coming out, try to help others hear them, amplify them, broadcast them. And so then the question was, well, what to do?"

One idea, made around the dinner table in Voices' North Side collective, was to assemble the statements and post them on the group's website. "We thought, let's just put them out there—

they speak for themselves, we don't need to say anything else," said Voices' Danny Muller.

And they had another idea: a walk from Washington, DC to New York, linking the two cities that had been most deeply affected by the tragedies. Voices had considered making such a walk before military action began in Afghanistan, but were unable to organize it before the bombing started. Re-energized by the statements from 9/11 family members, and bolstered by friends who urged that public witness against the war was still necessary, Voices organized the walk out of four faith-based communities where they already had strong connections: Washington, DC, Baltimore, Philadelphia, and New York. Speaking events and sleeping arrangements could be made in advance. They would be joined by members of allied organizations, including Veterans for Peace, Pax Christi, and War Resister's League.

A year earlier, Voices and the Middle East Children's Alliance had purchased an old school bus (with more than 400,000 miles on its odometer) and transformed it into a forty-foot-long rolling billboard and classroom to raise consciousness about the sanctions against Iraq. Complete with phone, computer, audio-visual aids, and thousands of printed handouts, it was used for a "Remembering Omran" bus tour, honoring Omran Harbi Jawair, a 13-year-old Iraqi shepherd boy who was killed by a U.S. missile strike in the southern no-fly zone as he was herding his family's flocks. After September 11, it was repainted colorfully with quotes from Reverend Martin Luther King, Jr. and the word "peace" in multiple languages. Informally dubbed "the rainbow bus," it was readied for the new tour.

Meanwhile, the collected statements on Voices' website started attracting attention. "We began to get calls like crazy from people wondering where we got them, and asking us how to reach them," Muller remembers. "And we said, 'We found these online, we don't have contacts for these people.'"

The family members themselves started searching the web, and discovered not only their own statements, but also statements from other families. Kelly Campbell and Barry Amundson had already begun reaching out to others, with the goal of organizing a coalition of families opposed to the war. At the same time, Potorti, unsettled by the thought that the country would be celebrating the holidays while celebrating war, imagined writing a joint letter, signed by 9/11 families opposing the military action, that could be read in front of the White House at Christmas. But he was clueless about how to organize it, and what, if anything, might come out of it.

He had seen several of the family members' statements in a press release issued by the Institute for Public Accuracy—a nationwide consortium of policy researchers providing alternative viewpoints and guests to the media—and called them for advice. Hearing that Potorti was a 9/11 family member, IPA communications director Sam Husseini told him about the Voices in the Wilderness walk. Word on the grapevine was that they were interested in having family members come along, and Husseini suggested that Potorti call their Chicago office. He imagined that he would be joining a host of other family members, and was surprised to find Voices' reaction to his offer of participation as somewhat muted.

"We really hadn't anticipated that family members would actually join in," said Kathy Kelly. "It was very difficult for us even to pick up the phone and make a 'cold call.' I remember being on a bus, going to some speaking engagement, working so hard over personal letters to each person, and never sending them. We really felt clutched, because you don't want to interrupt a family, or perhaps reach one family member and have that family member be in division or dissent with others, because of choosing this kind of an action. So the truth is, we didn't send out letters. Instead, we put the word out that we were very, very interested to hear from people."

At the same time, Barry Amundson's web searching located a Potorti essay, "Collateral Damage," written for the Durham, North Carolina newspaper, *The Independent Weekly*. Amundson e-mailed the newspaper, asking them to forward a note. "I commend David on his speaking out," Amundson wrote in solidarity, and he included a link to their family's essay. Potorti wrote back and mentioned the Voices walk, forwarding a proposed itinerary that had been sent from Chicago. Potorti said he was considering going, but truth be told, he didn't want to go unless others came along. Five days later, the Amundsons and Campbell also committed. With family members on board, Kelly shortened the original duration of the walk to one week: it would be difficult, not just physically, but emotionally, and public reaction—particularly in New York City—remained a bit of a wild card.

Each of them had their own reason for going. "It was kind of a memorial for me," Ryan Amundson said. "More than the National Memorial in Washington, DC on the one-month anniversary of the September 11 attack. At that event, President Bush and Donald Rumsfeld talked about 'eliminating evildoers.' They didn't say much about remembering the victims, and I thought that was the whole point of a memorial. It was like we were denied the memorial that we all deserved, because it was put in the context of perpetuating violence—that there was going to be more death, and a long, bloody road ahead of us. That didn't make me feel any better at all. It made me feel a lot worse."

TO HONOR THE VICTIMS
by Ryan Amundson
November 4, 2001

On September 11, my brother Craig was killed in the Pentagon. My family and I are devastated, but we are committed to dealing with our

Walk for Healing and Peace: Ryan Amundson meets the press

loss in a healthy way. It is easy to slide down the destructive path of anger, but in the long run this will only lead to more suffering. Focusing on revenge will never bring us comfort. Instead, we want to remember my brother and work on healing.

The September 11 attacks were not only a personal loss for my family, but a loss for our nation and the world. On this scale, it also takes a commitment to deal with this loss in a healthy, constructive way. Unfortunately, the United States has collectively taken the easy and destructive route of violent retaliation. Hopefully this will change.

On October 26, 2001, reporter Russell Mokhiber asked White House Spokesman Ari Fleischer about the President's response to the position of many victims' families who have spoken out against the Administration's violent response.

I am glad to see that our opposition is noticed, but I am disappointed at the response the White House spokesman gave. On behalf of the President, Ari Fleischer said, "The reason the United States, in the few times it has gone to war, has won every war it has ever fought, is because people are always free to express the thought that war is wrong, that war is bad, and the United States should not participate in it. And that is why we are a free country and a strong country. It is also the President's feeling that the actions he has taken help save lives, protect lives, and it is a war that we must fight for the next generation, for our children and grandchildren, so that they can live free from terror, and so that their families will not have to suffer from the murders that took place to the families . . ."

By implying that our opposition to the war will help him win the very war we speak out against, the President's response rides a line between nonsense and insult. It is also dismissive of our plea, and avoids any rational argument. Our position is characterized as one that opposes the President's actions based on "the thought that war is wrong, that war is bad, and the United States should not participate in it." This comment is as simplistic and absurd as a characterization of the Administration as having "the thought that war is right, that war is good, and the United States should participate in it." Our criticism of the war is not based on a rigid belief against all war.

Maybe we are misunderstood, so I'd like to clarify. We believe that war may be necessary in some circumstances, but in this circumstance, we believe that it is not. The violent actions of September 11 were a crime against humanity perpetrated by terrorists, not an act of war waged by any particular nation. Nonetheless, the U.S. has attacked an entire nation and the public is being primed for more to come.

We criticize our leader's response to the September 11 attacks because it will not effectively combat the root causes of terrorism and it is not likely to lead to true justice. The root causes of terrorism are not simply "evil people." People are not born evil. Instead, terrorism arises from social and economic conditions. The U.S. should work to prevent conditions which breed the hate and extremism necessary for such violent acts as experienced on September 11. We do not see how the current military response will stop terrorism.

Many have remarked that our bombing campaign in Afghanistan will actually make terrorist attacks more likely. Secretary of Defense Donald Rumsfeld even acknowledged the validity of this claim. The actions of the Administration have already killed hundreds of innocent people, perhaps more. If the bombing doesn't stop soon, millions will risk starvation this winter. What better recruitment tool for terrorist organizations could there be than a picture of a baby that died as a result of the indiscriminate actions of the United States? The bombing in Afghanistan will only fuel more hatred toward our country, making terrorist attacks more likely in the future. Aside from its inhumanity, the current strategy promoted by the Administration is counterproductive.

While we want to see a halt to the bombing and the death of more innocent people in Afghanistan, we also want those who conspired in the September 11 attacks to be justly punished. According to Ari Fleischer, the Administration is satisfied with whatever form justice takes through a military campaign. As the family of a victim of a violent crime, we feel that we have a right to see justice carried out in a recognized court of law, not on a battlefield. My idea of true justice is that which is carried out in a civilized manner. This form of justice is a benchmark of American society, a form of justice not likely found through a violent war. The Bush Administration should ensure that these principles of American justice are followed, even in the midst of fear and anger.

War is not the only option. The military campaign is not likely to bring the perpetrators to justice in a way that will make my family feel good, because it is killing innocent people and making terrorist attacks more likely in the future. It does not address the root causes of terrorism, only terrorists themselves. Although violent retaliation to a violent crime may seem appropriate, in the end it will only contribute to the cycle of violence. Not only is violent action not the only option, it is an option littered with pitfalls and hypocrisy.

Inaction is not the only alternative to violence. The United States could call for a tribunal on the crimes against humanity committed on September 11. We can also promote democracy and justice by halting all support of violent and oppressive regimes throughout the world, including the Northern Alliance. Striving for a world free from hate and terror doesn't necessarily mean using bombs and bullets. Alternatives to a violent war may not be as convenient for the President, but as the leader of the United States, his job is not an easy one.

Stopping terrorism requires fundamental social and economic changes. The current strategy of reliance on violent force does not address these essential aspects. The Bush Administration should concentrate more on exploring alternatives to an ineffective, counterproductive, and vengeful military campaign.

My family and I, among many other victims' families, plead with our leaders to formulate a just response to the terror of September 11. We ask that the President not exploit our nation's anger, but do his best to direct this energy toward constructive ends.

The greatest honor to my brother's life would be that his death would mark the end of this vicious cycle of violence. We hope that the President and the rest of our nation's leaders will find a way to honor all those who died on September 11 by responding to these atrocities in a healthy way. We beg our nation's leaders not to abide by the same ethical standards as the attackers on September 11, namely, the use of violence against innocent people. We want the bombing in Afghanistan to stop.

* * *

The Walk for Healing and Peace began November 25, 2001, at Georgetown University, moving past the Naval Observatory (home to the Vice President), through Kahlil Gibran Park, and past a life-sized statue of Mahatma Gandhi, with members of the group stopping to reflect and speak along the way. When they came to the White House, they were ordered by the police to keep moving if they wanted to stay there. Not wanting to leave, the group made a fairly ridiculous bow to federal regulations by marching in a circle.

The following day included a visit to Arlington National Cemetery, where Craig Amundson was buried. "It was really difficult to look down at his gravesite and feel that sense of loss, and then look around at all of these gravestones," said Ryan. "I

Walk for Healing and Peace, November 2001

thought, this is my personal situation, this is my life, and then realized that all of these people have been affected by war in some way. We kind of broke down and cried in front of everybody, and everybody else was crying. It made the walk really personal for all of us."

At its largest, the walk totaled about thirty people. They quickly bonded, and got into a routine of riding the rainbow bus into a town, walking, vigiling, speaking, and interacting with the press. "Every day, it was like going on a stage without rehearsing your lines," Barry Amundson said. "We were doing it for ourselves, and because it needed to be done, regardless of the media, or who was there."

The walk continued through Baltimore, Maryland; Chester, Pennsylvania, home of the Calvary Baptist Church where Martin Luther King, Jr. once served as an Associate Pastor; and Philadelphia, the birthplace of freedom, where their actions were confined to the inner perimeter of a white box—designated as the acceptable "free speech" area were signs could be held and leaflets distributed—painted on the sidewalk near the historic Liberty Bell.

They vigiled at Philadelphia City Hall, where the mayor's

annual Christmas tree lighting attracted large crowds—as well as one thousand protesters opposed to school privatization. They walked through the streets of Montclair, New Jersey, carrying signs reading, *"Our Grief is Not a Cry for War,"* and *"No More Victims,"* while handing out fliers opposing the war in Afghanistan. For the family members, who had never really participated in public demonstrations, it was a whole new world.

"Most people along their route showed curiosity, accepting the fliers and smiling, perhaps more at the novelty of a demonstration marching through town than out of support for the group's views," wrote a reporter for the *Montclair Times*, accurately capturing the mood of the day. One passerby offered high-fives while admitting he could never have the courage to do what

Voices in the Wilderness' Kathy Kelly inside the rainbow bus

the marchers were doing. A woman driving by in a car yelled out of her window, "What, let them come here and kill all of us?" If fear was in the air, one had to remember that of the 662 New Jersey residents—one quarter of those lost at the World Trade Center—the biggest percentage came from this area.

"For every insult or obscenity that we heard, we had fifteen or twenty cars going by, honking their horns, giving us a thumbs-up or a peace sign, people just thanking us for what we were doing," Ryan Amundson said. "On the one hand, there was hostility, and on the other, there was receptivity, because people were feeling just really hopeless about what's going on."

The walk continued through Jersey City, Patterson, and Caldwell, New Jersey. At St. Dominic Academy, a Catholic girls school, Potorti and Voices' Joe Proulx made a joint presentation. "I talked about the long-term consequences of terrorism and war, my dad's military experiences, and some family friends who survived the Auschwitz concentration camp, and Joe went on to talk about UN sanctions and how they were decimating the children in Iraq," Potorti said. "We asked for questions, and this girl says, 'Why should we spend money on kids in Iraq, when kids in Jersey City are getting shot in the street?' That really summed it up for me, the economics of it. All this money going to the military, while cities are falling apart, and kids are having to duke it out with each other for what's left. I thought, what is going to happen to all these children?"

As the group made its way into New York City on December 1—riding the ferry from Staten Island to lower Manhattan in full view of the gaping hole in the skyline—they were keenly aware of respecting the mood there. There was, in fact, some fear about how the delegation would be received. "We should all remember that along the walk we may be able to do some teaching, but that once we get into New York City, we will do the learning," Kathy Kelly told them.

Other peace marchers were waiting as the ferry docked. Among them was Frances Anderson, an actress who in the role of Rabbi Deena Golden gave spiritual solace to her costars on the soap opera, *The Guiding Light*. In the real world, she had decided to document participants in the emerging antiwar movement—to what end, she had yet to determine—and heard about the walk by visiting the American Friends Service Committee

(AFSC) website. She followed and interviewed the family members for the entire weekend, at first expecting their story to be only one part of her video.

"Those two days of taping the events around the walk in Manhattan were such a moving experience for me," Anderson said, "that from that point on, I decided to focus my documentary on the core group of September 11 family members." Their meeting at the ferry would mark the beginning of a long friendship with Peaceful Tomorrows.

The delegation made its way up lower Broadway, carrying signs reading, *"Break the Cycle of Violence,"* and *"Justice, not Just War."* While hearing occasional remarks of disbelief, along with observations that "the sixties are over," their passage was given a subdued reception by the people so closely affected by the terrorist attacks, or else went largely unnoticed. It was a mild Saturday for December, and proved to be a busy shopping day. The hustle and bustle of the crowded sidewalks was positively surreal: One could pause next to a street vendor selling CDs or scarves, only to look up and see the last skeletal remains of the destroyed towers a block away. "How can they be shopping?" Potorti mused,

Approaching lower Manhattan

wondering how life could have returned so quickly to the mundane in the shadow of those towers. It was the first time he had visited New York since September 11.

"We looked at each other and he said, 'I think I'm feeling now what you must have felt when you stood before the Pentagon,'" Ryan said of Potorti. "And I could see in his eyes—especially for him, because people's bodies weren't being identified—the feeling that you want to just reach out and grab onto the building and pull your loved one close to you. It was extremely difficult to think about the violence, and the fact that they're bulldozing these buildings, and that as families we still have not had a chance to even process what's going on. And for some, not having an opportunity to put their loved one to rest . . . it's horrible."

One family member walked with an American flag draped over her shoulders. "I thought it was important to show people that we're patriotic," Ryan said. "That you can be asking for alternatives to what the government is doing right now and still

Remains of the World Trade Center

be patriotic. It was important for us to really put that American flag in a context of peace, rather than in a context of war."

The group walked to Union Square Park—the site of enormous vigils as well as antiwar demonstrations in the days and weeks after the attacks, and squared off for the first time with the New York media: 1010 WINS News Radio, *New York Daily News, New York Post,* and *New York Times.* These media outlets were largely receptive and respectful, as were the crowds that formed as the group made a circle and shared public witness to the purpose of their walk. Manhattanite Susan Sarandon chanced upon the gathering and expressed her pleasure at locating the group, whose progress had been chronicled on Pacifica's *Democracy Now.* Such small gestures of solidarity meant a lot to the group's morale.

The following morning, the *New York Times* printed a photo in its "Portraits of Grief" section featuring the group—but notably cropping out enough of their signs to render the antiwar messages unreadable. Potorti would write a letter to the editor, explaining,

> While the *Times* was accurate in depicting our presence at a "vigil," it did not show the signs we carried, or mention that the vigil was the culmination of an eight-day walk for healing and peace . . . Our motive, and that of our fellow marchers, was to seek alternatives to war as a response to our personal and national tragedies. While your photographer did a great job, we did not come to New York to get our picture taken. We came to demand an end to the war in Afghanistan.

The *Times* did not run the letter. It did, however, run a correction about the photo caption, saying that it "described the event incompletely. It marked the end of an eight-day peace march from Washington to New York."

Sunday, December 2, marked the final leg of the peace walk. Gathering at Cadman Plaza in Brooklyn Heights, the group joined with local peace activists to walk over the Brooklyn Bridge at sunset. The winter sky was brilliant red and strikingly beauti-

The rainbow bus at Cadman Plaza, Brooklyn

ful. The magical skyline of Manhattan, however—which from this vantage point looked like the Emerald City in *The Wizard of Oz*—remained notable for the absence of the Towers. The group marched through Greenwich Village and on to St. Francis Xavier Church. A crowd of seventy-five heard family members and others from the walk speak on issues of war and peace. It was here that the group met Colleen Kelly.

Kelly happened to hear about the walk from friends at the Catholic Worker House in North Philadelphia, who she called for details about an upcoming annual meeting of the Catholic Conference of Bishops. She wanted to send them a letter telling her story and encouraging them to oppose the war in Afghanistan. Kelly was a pious Irish Catholic and deeply conflicted about the war. She wanted her family to be safe. But she knew that war was not the answer.

"One stumbling block seems to be the lack of choices given the American public concerning our response to 9/11," she wrote to Thomas Gumbleton, an outspoken bishop from Detroit known for his commitment to nonviolence. "Our country sees no other way because we have been presented with no other way. This is my urgent request of the bishops: Can you begin a discussion of the other way, Christ's way? Could you help provide moral guidance to a majority that is voicing support for a bombing campaign, but with reserve and ambivalence? Could you open a dialogue of alternatives—concrete ideas leading to Christ's truth in our hearts? Could you pray that we may all be open to God's difficult and sometimes divisive message?" (Later, a majority of the bishops—Gumbleton not among them—would vote to support the military action.)

Kelly read from her letter that night at St. Francis Xavier's, and she and the group immediately saw in each other like-minded spirits.

"I still find it difficult to express how I felt meeting the group," Kelly said. "My family was this huge support system for me, but there was something missing, an integral part of me that still needed healing. Through meeting the group, that healing started to happen. It was very powerful and affirming. I was feeling so alone, and hadn't been able to verbalize much of what I was feeling, but the group gave me a way to do that."

After a closing song and some conversation, the family group turned to one last piece of business. They made their way to the historic White Horse Tavern—notable as the bar where poet Dylan Thomas drank himself to death—to talk about the next day's press conference summarizing their experiences on the walk. Over beers, the Amundsons, Campbell, Potorti, and Kelly, who was joined by her husband, Dan, brainstormed what would later become many of the central goals of Peaceful Tomorrows, claiming them as rights:

9/11 Family Members Joint Statement
December 2, 2001

We are claiming our right to demand that alternatives to war be considered, explored, and enacted;

Notes from the White Horse, December 2, 2001

Claiming our right to demand that the violence being perpetrated in Afghanistan not be done in our name;

Claiming our right to demand that perpetrators of the horrible crimes of September 11 be brought to justice in an open court of law, in the full light of day, subject to the rights that we cherish and share;

Claiming our right to reject revenge as a response to our deeply personal family tragedies;

Claiming our right to spare innocent families in Afghanistan and other nations from feeling the pain and loss that we have felt in our own families;

Claiming our right to express a common bond with other innocent victims of terrorism and tragedy all over the world without being labeled unpatriotic or un-American;

As proud Americans, we are claiming our right to not be surveilled, censored, or punished for exercising our Constitutional rights of free speech;

Claiming our right to prevent this war from expanding endlessly into nation after nation with no oversight or input from the American people;

We are announcing, loudly and clearly, that after making this eight-day Walk for Healing and Peace, we know we are not alone in making these claims;

And we invite family members of other 9/11 victims to contact us.

The next morning, they printed the joint statement, along with a press release and some biographical information, and headed back to Union Square Park for their press conference.

CNN and the New York City Fox News affiliate were the sole representatives of the "fourth estate" to appear, graciously instructing the group on where to stand for optimal effect. As the rest of the group held up a large American flag, Potorti read the joint statement to a scattering of bemused onlookers seated on park benches.

The Fox producer, who had expressed an interest in interviewing the participants one-on-one, had a difference of opinion with the cameraman, who stalked off. The event never aired on either network. The group repaired to the B&H Dairy—a Lower East Side hole-in-the-wall serving homemade soup—which they would later learn was only blocks away from the apartment of Rita Lasar—whom none of them had met at the time. And thus was held the first press conference by the people who would later found Peaceful Tomorrows.

I have read many of the statements made by family members of those lost in Sept. They are eloquent and profound and I just wanted to say how sorry I am for your loss and "thank you" for having the courage and the strength to speak out and say what needs to be heard. It is noble that in the midst of your own pain, you are reaching out to try to keep others from experiencing the same thing.
—E-mail to Walk For Healing and Peace group,
December 2001

Chapter Four

Before they went their separate ways, there was consensus among the family members that they'd like to keep going. It had been good to speak out. It had also been scary, and sad, and bittersweet. And most of all, it was impossible to imagine doing it alone.

Campbell investigated routes by which they could organize as a group, a process made easier by the fact that she already worked for a nonprofit. A cold call to the Ford Foundation landed her a next-day meeting with a vice president and senior staff, who encouraged her that foundations would be supportive of building a coalition of family members committed to speaking out. Global Exchange, a San Francisco–based human rights group, had contacted Ryan after seeing an e-mail exchange with one of his college professors. They had an intriguing idea: They were thinking about taking a 9/11 family delegation to Afghanistan.

But it was the Fellowship of Reconciliation's Janet Chisholm, one of the oganization's nonviolence trainers, who made the offer they were looking for. FOR, based in Nyack, New York, was the oldest peace and justice group in the United States, formed in 1915 to counsel World War I conscientious objectors, and later "birthing" groups like the ACLU. Chisholm, in consultation with the rest of the organization, proposed that FOR would serve as "interim fiscal sponsor" for the family members if they wanted to launch their own organization. That meant they could collect donations, pay their phone bills, and stay on the right side of the IRS until they organized more formally.

Chisholm had heard about the family members from Kathy Kelly, who suggested giving them nonviolence training before the Walk for Healing and Peace. Scheduling conflicts had prevented her from doing so, but she continued to see their action as consistent with FOR's mission. "Each of them was taking a stance against retaliation and vengeance," Chisholm said. "I call that transformative nonviolence: taking action, taking risk, stepping out and taking initiatives in response to violence and injustice. It's action that transforms yourself and your opponent—and 'changes the script.' I saw them doing that very powerfully, and saw that people were ready to listen to them."

The AFSC also weighed in. Kevin Heffel—hired to coordinate a September 11 Peace Response Project for six months out of the organization's New York office—had time to devote to the nascent group. And in Washington, DC, Kate Lowenstein, National Organizer for Murder Victims Families for Reconciliation—an organization of family members opposed to the death penalty—shared tips that would prove invaluable as the group evolved: have a clear message; be prepared for controversy; work independently from other groups; be careful to say you don't represent all 9/11 families; and fill staff and board positions with family members to keep focus and control.

As the holidays approached, the group remained in constant phone and e-mail contact. Campbell proposed basic structural necessities for the imagined group, including "goals" and a "mission statement." She and Potorti edited the group's barroom brainstorms and passed them around for further massaging by the others. By mid-December 2001, they were also kicking around ideas for a group name: *Families for True Justice; 9/11 Just Response Network; Breaking the Cycle; 9/11 Families for Effective Action; 9/11 Families Against Terrorism; Reason Over Revenge; 9/11 Families for a Safer World; 9/11 Families for Effective Action Against Terrorism; 9/11 Families for a Comprehensive Response; Victims' Families Seeking Due Process; Survivors for Effective Action Against Terrorism; Victims' Families Against War; Stopping Terror with Other Plans; Mourners Organizing to Effectively Stop Terror; Just Alternatives; Good Relations; Related to Peace; Peace is Relative;* and *Families Choose Peace.*

"Choose your top three favorites," Campbell instructed via e-mail. "Hopefully, there will be some overlap." There wasn't. There were concerns: What about people who had lost friends, rather than family, and what about people who hadn't lost anyone but still wanted to support them? How could they all be included? Should they have "families" in the name? What about people who didn't have kids? How could they be sure to include victims of terrorism from other countries? So the names continued to float.

It was while going through a book of quotations from Martin Luther King, Jr., edited by Coretta Scott King, that Potorti noticed an excerpt from a speech made in 1967 about the Vietnam War:

> The past is prophetic in that it asserts loudly that wars are poor chisels for carving out peaceful tomorrows. One day we must come to see that peace is not merely a distant goal that we seek, but a means by which we arrive at that goal. We must pursue peaceful ends through peaceful means. How much longer must we play at deadly war games before we heed the plaintive pleas of the unnumbered dead and maimed of past wars?

Potorti threw "peaceful tomorrows" into the mix. It was more metaphorical than the others, much less "on the nose" in describing the group. Maybe that would shake things up. They could extend it to read "September 11th Families for Peaceful Tomorrows" to make it clearer.

Lasar and her kids thought it was the dumbest thing they had ever heard. Potorti ran it by a friend in the advertising business who said that Peaceful Tomorrows "sounds like a flavor of Celestial Seasonings tea." The comment was off-putting, but Potorti decided they might be on to something: What could be more mainstream than the cozy boxes of tea with the historical quotes, and wouldn't it be nice if they could actually cut a promotional deal with Celestial Seasonings?

He started championing the name, and in what was to become a typical process—due to geographic distance and distraction—the group couldn't come to a decision. An e-mail from Ryan about Peaceful Tomorrows finally broke the log jam: "We've got a good one here, let's go for it." And thus, whether through default or exhaustion, the name was chosen.

* * *

The holidays, starting with Thanksgiving, had been as difficult as everyone anticipated, and got worse as December wore on. But this was mitigated by outpourings of support, not only from friends and family but also from complete strangers.

"Handmade quilts, Christmas ornaments, and cards from strangers kept arriving," Campbell reported. At the family assistance center near the World Trade Center site, where donated items were available, Colleen Kelly picked up a toddler's firefighter outfit—yellow slicker, boots, and hat—and sent it to Potorti's son. The generosity directed not only to family members, but to those still struggling with clean-up and recovery efforts at the site, was beyond description.

Still, it was hard to handle the losses—of not just their loved ones, but their peace of mind, their certainty about the future, and their sense of control over events. These were not unique feelings for family members, or for the public in general, but were amplified by the unfamiliar experience of going public with unconventional views. "This is my first minority experience," Potorti said about the reception given his views in some quarters.

Like the others, he continued to do media interviews as Christmas approached. Some were with sympathetic talk radio hosts like the i.e. America Radio Network's Mike Malloy and the American Urban Radio Network's Bev Smith. Others, like Fox News' Bill O'Reilly, were more skeptical.

Potorti hadn't watched television in years, didn't have cable, and had never seen *The O'Reilly Factor.* But he knew that he'd be criticized. And he knew that he didn't have to go on the show. But he made a realization about himself that he would come to characterize as "having nothing left to lose." His brother was dead. His family would never be the same again. Why not take a stand against the war, even if he wound up looking stupid and got phone calls from crazy people? The tragedy had given him, and the others, a kind of freedom.

During Potorti's December 19 appearance, O'Reilly compared the Taliban to Hitler and the Afghan people to the German people: Weren't the Germans responsible for Hitler? So aren't the Afghan people responsible for the Taliban? And shouldn't we take them out, just as we did the German people in World War II? "You need to rethink this," he demanded. "We had to defeat these people with as few casualties as possible. That's why we bombed."

The logic was equally profound on right-wing talk radio. Appearing via phone on an AM outlet in San Diego, callers compared Potorti with "traitor" John Walker, while another inquired if he wanted to "kiss Osama on the lips." After his microphone was cut during the show's wrap-up, in which the host concluded that not a single person had been "killed" in Afghanistan (since we were acting in self-defense), Potorti unloaded on the show's producer.

"I don't get to respond to that bullshit diatribe?" he asked. The producer said she had given Potorti an hour for his "agenda." Agenda? "Oh yeah," she replied, "I think you're a peace activist from way back. Your brother gets killed, and you've got your moment in the spotlight, and you're riding it for all it's worth."

That she would also express concern that her own children "not get killed"—the suggestion being that peace activists were making that possibility more, not less, likely—was more to the point. Behind the anger directed at them, Potorti and the others would come to learn, there was always fear. And fear was in big supply as 2001 drew to a close.

* * *

The approach of the new year also brought with it a sense of urgency on the part of Medea Benjamin. She was the co-founder of Global Exchange, the nonprofit dedicated to "creating people-to-people ties"—or, as she explains it, "taking people out of their own small circles and showing them other circles." Participants could take "reality tours" to live with Central American coffee growers; to meet with South Africans who successfully ended political apartheid; or to meet Mexican peasants fighting for a piece of land. If the group was going to bring a delegation of family members to Afghanistan, it would have to be soon. Public interest in the war was winding down, and the press was pulling up stakes.

Like Kathy Kelly of Voices in the Wilderness, Benjamin had been moved by the public statements of the family members. " I thought these voices have to be elevated," she said. "These voices have to be on the major talk shows, they have to be the experts in how you fight terrorism." But the idea of taking a delegation to

Afghanistan didn't occur to her until Global Exchange actually went to the region in mid-November, at the height of the bombing campaign, visiting seven refugee camps just over the Afghanistan border in Pakistan. It became clear that there were countless innocent victims, and that they were in desperate need of help.

Returning to the States, Benjamin quickly learned that her message—there's a lot of people hurting as a result of the bombing, and they need our help—was not resonating with the U.S. media. Only one TV camera showed up at Global Exchange's press conference, even though they were the first American delegation to return from the region since the bombing began. Civilian casualties of any kind were denied on a daily basis; bombs were "smart," precision-guided, and never missed their mark. The only TV network that expressed an interest was the Washington, DC outpost of Al-Jazeera—whose Kabul, Afghanistan offices had been bombed by the United States.

The family members, meanwhile, had been driven to speak out because of their concern for Afghan civilians, but didn't know how to help. Campbell remembers talking to Colleen Kelly on the phone in December, brainstorming about what could be done.

"You're going to think I'm crazy," Kelly said, "but what if we could go to Afghanistan ourselves?"

Back in the San Francisco Bay Area, Barry Amundson called Jason Mark, Media Director at Global Exchange. Mark had already been helping the Amundsons by passing along the names of other September 11 families he had located through the media. Campbell and Amundson met him for lunch to solicit his advice about creating a family group. He told them about Medea Benjamin's idea to return to Afghanistan—if there were September 11 family members willing to go with her.

The Amundsons, Campbell, Potorti, and Kelly expressed

conditional interest and agreed to have a conference call with Benjamin the day after Christmas. But after spending the holiday with their families, their enthusiasm went missing. It was a dicey security situation. Their families had already lost one loved one and were heartsick at the thought of losing another. Benjamin began to lose confidence. But there was still Lasar, who met the others on the phone for the first time that day.

"When I called other people, there would be this long silence after I explained why it was so important to go to Afghanistan, and the logical question that followed was, 'What's the security situation like?'" Benjamin recalled. "And I couldn't say this was a piece of cake—it's a dangerous place. But with Rita, there was a long silence, and then with her raspy New York voice, she says, 'Can I smoke in Afghanistan?' And it was so wonderful, because it was the moment that I knew this trip was going to happen: Rita's going to go, and she's going to get other people to go."

Derrill Bodley, whom Benjamin learned about after reading an article in the *San Francisco Chronicle*, was also contacted. But she found his thinking about the appropriateness of the Afghanistan bombing to be more nuanced.

"My daughter was on a plane were the passengers took action," Bodley said. "So I had this mix of emotions going on, having to do with people who take action against threats of some kind. I was also considering the 'just war' theory, but didn't have a clear idea about what that philosophy was. Before I was going to renounce war as a vehicle for achieving an end, I wanted to know more. I thought it was a little less productive to focus on trying to stop this war than on trying to emphasize the alternatives to war in general."

When it came to the question of joining the delegation, there was one problem: On Christmas day, Bodley had checked himself into the hospital with stress-related symptoms mimicking a heart attack. His wife would be a wreck if he did this. He was a music teacher and was committed to a class schedule. He said he'd consider it a few months later, but not now. Benjamin decided not to push him.

The next day, Lasar called her. She'd been doing a crossword puzzle, and happened to read her horoscope, which she summarized as follows: "You're about to embark on a significant journey that will have a profound impact. Your fellow travelers don't quite understand how profound this journey is, but a pep talk from you will make the difference." She asked for Derrill's phone number. She called and told him a hundred reasons why he shouldn't go to Afghanistan and one reason why he should: his daughter. Bodley had already been thinking the same thing, and he finally agreed to go. Derrill's stepdaughter, Eva Rupp, who was familiar with Global Exchange from taking a "reality tour" years earlier, also made a commitment, as did Campbell. A delegation of family members would be going to Afghanistan.

*I think it comes down to simply building human relation-
ships with people here. Just making each other understand
that we're human beings and we're basically the same.
Even though we come from a really different country, we
have different religions, we're really the same in a lot of
ways. Everybody loves their children. Everybody wants
good lives for themselves. Everybody wants peace.*
—Eva Rupp in Afghanistan, January 2002

Chapter Five

If Medea Benjamin had any concerns about press attention
being brought to bear on the plight of the Afghan people, they
ceased when the UN plane landed in Afghanistan on January
15, 2002. "We saw this sea of press, and we were just aston-
ished," she said. "At first we thought, that can't be for us, that's
got to be for somebody else. We had heard that Colin Powell was
on his way to Afghanistan, so maybe an Air Force plane just
landed right behind us. Or maybe it was Bono or Madonna or
somebody really famous. And then we realized that it was for
our delegation."

There was no denying it: This was a unique story, one that
went against the grain of conventional wisdom and, some might
suggest, common sense—people whose families had been ripped
apart in the worst act of terrorism on U.S. soil had just arrived in
the alleged backyard of the terrorists. They were here, in person,
to break bread with their counterparts—civilians who had lost
family members in the crossfire. If the U.S. press was reluctant to
question the efficacy of the bombing campaign, or the public's
support for it, the arrival of the delegation created an opportunity
to examine those issues from a variety of new angles.

And it was not just the U.S. press—it was the European and
the Latin American press, Univision and Telemundo; the

Japanese press; and the Arab press, Al-Jazeera and reporters from Abu Dhabi, Indonesia, and Malaysia. Jacquie Soohen, a New York documentarian with Big Noise Films, a nonprofit, all-volunteer collective of media-makers from around the world, would document their journey and make her footage available for the group's use. The first problem on the ground became how to balance these herds of press with the "intimate" meetings planned among family members and Afghans in their small homes.

As the media swept in, a British soldier was dispatched to help Campbell locate a missing piece of luggage. Their few moments of quiet from the press gave her an opportunity to explain who the group was and why they had come.

"He was silent for a minute," Campbell said, "and then he asked, 'What do you think about the way they are taking the detainees to Guantánamo?' As a soldier, he was worried that this apparent break with Geneva conventions could have negative implications for himself and his fellow soldiers on the ground in Afghanistan: If we weren't treating the enemy fairly, why would they be compelled to treat our soldiers fairly? His point brought home the fact that, even while the world seemed united behind the war on terrorism, there were quiet concerns and questions being raised by those most affected by the policies."

It remained an exceedingly difficult trip. As they drove to the capital city of Kabul, they saw old ruined Soviet tanks sitting on the side of the road. Craters of varying sizes dotted the sad landscape. Old, unexploded ordinance from previous wars, along with fresh U.S. cluster "bomblets"—the 202 small shrapnel bombs that fan out from each cluster bomb—were everywhere. The buildings that remained standing looked like crumbling sandcastles. In Kabul, there were no post offices, banks, or working telephones. Electricity came and went with no rhyme or reason. In the whole city there were only a handful of restaurants, and they were all in pretty bad shape. The best hotel in town, the

Kelly Campbell, Derrill Bodley, and Medea Benjamin
visit with children at Internally Displaced Person's camp

Intercontinental, didn't have sheets, hot water, or even running water, in most of the rooms. Dust was everywhere, turning everyone's hands black, but there was no water to wash them. The delegation quickly developed what was known as the "Kabul cough," from the dry, dusty air.

Using Global Exchange's contacts on the ground, the group visited the homes of Afghan civilians directly affected by the bombing campaign—which was continuing in the eastern part of the country. In one house, so many members of the press were present that arguments broke out among camera people blocking each other's shots. An elderly Afghan man with a bullet wound was pushed off a cushion in his own home by reporters trying to get better angles. Rupp was stepped on—twice—and left in frustration. As the novelty of the family members' visit waned among the mainstream U.S. press, it was the foreign media that stayed engaged to get the deeper story.

The trip is remembered in images. Nine- and ten-year-old siblings, a boy and a girl, whose house had been partially destroyed by a bomb, stopped talking. Shaking and drooling, wetting their beds, they were not able to sleep from nightmares. Wide-eyed children in hospitals were missing limbs due to cluster bombs. A woman four months pregnant, buried in the rubble of her bombed home, survived with horrific head injuries. A five-year-old girl was killed when a nearby bomb explosion collapsed a concrete vestibule in her apartment building, crushing her.

"I was naïve in the days before October 7, 2001," Bodley admitted. "I actually thought, and I said a little prayer, that if the war starts, please let there be no civilian casualties. That's where I was coming from—an uninformed and naïve position, thinking in idealistic terms, thinking about alternatives to war in general. And then, when I got to Afghanistan, the particulars of the situation were brought home quite strongly. I became aware of the reality that any war is going to cause these problems, and that we should prevent war at all costs."

Bodley was taken to the home of a woman who, like him, had lost a 20-year-old child. "I looked in her eyes, and that gave me chills," he said. "I couldn't hug her because it's not the kind of thing that you do, and I couldn't really say much to her because I didn't speak her language, so the only way to communicate was with the eyes. And it was moving, because eye contact can be overwhelming sometimes. I heard her through her eyes."

"Every single Afghan that I have met has the same eyes," said Lasar. "They're big, and beautiful, and sad. The three-year-olds, the 15-year-olds, the 23-year-olds. And it's interesting, the older people do not have that sadness because there was a time when they could remember peace." She refers to a time before decades of war and occupation by the Russians and the Taliban. "Nobody who is 23 or younger can remember one moment of peace. Not one. They're beautiful people and they have never, ever had a moment's peace."

Yalda, age 17, gets a kiss from Rita Lasar at the Alfatha school;
Yalda and her classmates wrote cards to American students

Even so, many of the Afghans they met proved to be exceptionally forgiving. As they bemoaned the deaths of their children, their parents, and their friends, they expressed gratitude for being freed from the Taliban. They acknowledged that the U.S. didn't purposely bomb them. And although they were living in miserable conditions made even worse by the military action, they retained a reservoir of compassion for those affected by 9/11.

Rita Lasar visited the Kabul home of Amin Said, who lost his brother and sister-in-law and most of their house in the U.S. bombing. As reported by Mark Landler in a *New York Times* article entitled, *"Sharing Grief to Find Understanding,"* Lasar told him about losing her brother on 9/11, and her hope for the Afghan victims:

> "We didn't mean to hurt you the way we did, but now we have to help you," Lasar said as she entered the Said home, where new walls and windows had erased the bomb's destruction. Clasping her hands and drawing her into a sun-filled room of cushions and carpets, Said told Lasar: "He was your brother, but he was also my brother. We are all brothers and sisters."

Dear kids of USA.

Hello, dears, we recieved your letters thanks a lot.

We are very sorry for september 11th situation in your beutiful country. As you might know, the same situations reppeatedly happend in our country since almost 20 years.

We have lost our parrents, our brothers, sisters, the bloody 20 years war killed thousands of our people, among them the number of children are much more than the others, Accept our greetings, Pleuse do not forget us we are with you.

SINCERLY yours
Hangama omer

Letter to American students from Hangama Omer at the Alfatha School, January 2002

"The amazing thing about all of those families was that they felt so much sympathy for us," Campbell said. "I'd pull out my pictures of Craig and our family, and some of them would go back and pull out a dog-eared picture they had of their child, or whoever was lost. There were times when we cried together. And there were families who said, 'Your loss is my loss.' We were able to transcend the cultural barriers, and transcend the language barriers, and make that connection—understanding what the other was going through, on a really basic human level. Even beyond the families who had lost someone to U.S. bombing, everyone we met in Kabul was easier to talk to about our losses than people in the United States, because everyone there knows what it's like. Everyone we met had a story about their own family member or their own loved one being tortured, being killed by violence in war. It was such a relief to meet people who knew exactly what to say to you, who didn't look at you with the kind of scared, blank stare that you get from a lot of people in the United States—people who are very well-meaning, but don't know what it feels like. All of those people knew what it felt like."

The delegation met a woman named Arifah who had been visiting a relative with her son when her home was destroyed by a bomb, killing her husband and the rest of her family. Her neighbor wrote an English-language letter to the U.S. government explaining what had happened: Since the United States was a friend of the Afghan people, and since this was clearly a mistake, and since she had nowhere else to go, couldn't the United States help her? She went to the U.S. embassy in Kabul to deliver the letter but was turned away at the gate as a "beggar."

They decided to organize a press conference at the embassy, where Arifah was invited to tell her story to the international media. The family members contrasted her treatment with the outpouring of love and support they had received from the world following September 11. Lasar then took Arifah's letter—along with claim forms the delegation had begun using to document civilian casualties—and handed them to a U.S. military guard. It was a symbolic gesture, to be sure, but it represented a much broader call: that America should not only acknowledge unintended civilian casualties, but should weigh them in making decisions to wage future wars. After much discussion, the delegation called for an Afghan victims fund to be approved by Congress.

The family members' visit proved to be a genuine catalyst for media coverage of Afghan civilians. Mainstream journalists on the ground, including those from the U.S., were largely sympathetic to the plight of the Afghan people and wanted to highlight their suffering, but couldn't get the stories past their editors. The presence of Americans, particularly September 11 family members, proved to be the human element—or more specifically, the *U.S.* human element—they were looking for. *"Afghan Plight: Tom Newton Dunn Talks to U.S. Victim's Sister in Kabul,"* read one torturously constructed headline in the *London Mirror. "Afghan Journey Eases a Father's Pain,"* read an *LA Times* article, comparing Bodley's grief with that of an Afghan father who also lost his child. Given the diligence with which the U.S. government was denying Afghan civilian casualties at the time, the coverage the delegation received in virtually every major mainstream newspaper in the U.S., along with appearances on CNN, Fox News, and other networks, were remarkable breakthroughs.

Still, the stories didn't always pan out. "A sympathetic reporter from *People* magazine wanted to do a story on us, but her editor said it was too political," Campbell recalls. "So they ended up doing a story on the lion at the Kabul zoo—which seems a little ironic, because it's supposed to be 'People' magazine. Here we are, a people-to-people delegation, and they do a story on a cuddly lion, which actually died several days later."

But there was no way to avoid the political context of the delegation. In a *New Zealand Herald* article entitled, *"U.S. Jittery at Symbolic Meetings of Grieving Families,"* Kim Sengupta wrote, "The meeting is seen by the grieving Americans as a step toward building something good out of profoundly shattering events. But they also bring with them a message of reconciliation that has provoked apprehension in the State Department and among U.S. diplomats in Afghanistan."

In fact, the U.S. embassy had just reopened, and was digging out from the debris of fifteen years of inactivity. The delegation met with acting ambassador Ryan Crocker, who told the family members that they could bring documentation of Afghans needing assistance after being affected by the U.S. military campaign—and that he was not aware of any such need.

While the delegation was in Kabul, several groups of U.S. legislators and Secretary of State Colin Powell also made visits to the city, usually for one day, some simply landing at Bagram Air Base for a press conference and then leaving, others spending their time inside the heavily guarded embassy. The family members, though, walked the streets freely, in many ways acting as the real ambassadors of the American people.

They were, however, not allowed to attend a Kabul press conference with Senator Tom Daschle, although a reporter from *USA Today* offered to raise the question of creating an Afghan Victims Fund. Daschle said that such a fund seemed like a reasonable part of an overall U.S. aid package to Afghanistan. The story featuring his remarks never made it into the paper.

As the family members prepared to depart, Powell, the first U.S. Secretary of State to visit the country since 1976, announced, "We are here to stay. We are committed to the future of this country."

In November 2002, General Richard Myers would admit to the *Washington Post* that the U.S. had "lost a little momentum" in the war in Afghanistan, and that it may be time for the military to "flip" its priorities to "the reconstruction piece." The same article would quote a CIA report stating, "Reconstruction may be the single most important factor in increasing security throughout Afghanistan and preventing it from again becoming a haven for terrorists."

Three months later, President Bush would submit a budget to Congress with exactly *zero* dollars earmarked for rebuilding Afghanistan.

AFGHANISTAN MEMORIES
by Rita Lasar

As we approached the Bagram Air Base, outside of Kabul, it seemed to me that I was landing on the surface of the moon. There appeared to be nothing but rubble and light brown dust as far as the eye could see. A pall came over me. I did not believe that it was possible to feel more sadness and disorientation than I had been experiencing since my brother perished in the World Trade Center on September 11, but here I was, in a country I had never imagined feeling connected to, experiencing the same shock as I had on that fateful day.

As I walked down the staircase of the UN plane that had brought me there, I realized that the symmetry between the events of September 11 and October 7 was almost complete. The drive to the city revealed more destruction and devastation than this privileged American had ever imagined. This was not a picture-book landscape or a television documentary. This was the reality of war.

In the car to the city, our guide pointed to a collapsed building, and told me that it had been a mosque recently bombed by my country. I asked if we could stop the car, for there before me was a sight identical, except in size, to what I had seen at Ground Zero a few days earlier. The metal frame of the mosque was sticking out of the structure at the exact angle the metal frame of the North Tower, the building my brother had died in, had protruded.

It was then that I fully understood why I had chosen to make this journey. I was to be a witness to the sorrow, horror, and suffering of the innocent people who were being made to pay for the September 11 attacks.

On the night we arrived in Kabul, after stopping at the guesthouse we would call home, Medea Benjamin and I rushed to the Intercontinental Hotel. One of the networks had given us a room there, so that I could be present for an interview early the next morning. There was a reason for our haste: Kabul was under total curfew, requiring us to arrive before it took effect. Guards along the way stopped our car, first to see if we had arms or other dangerous items, and then to see if they recognized the driver who was transporting these strange passengers.

I had been traveling for three full days to get here, and had slept in three different airports without showers. In Islamabad, Pakistan, I had finally slept on a bed, but it was not easy getting used to armed guards in the lobby and the entrance of the guesthouse. In short, I was completely worn out. When we arrived at the Intercontinental, the men behind the desk spoke no English. But they did manage to convey the fact that there was no room for us—no room, in fact, for anyone.

I decided—or rather, it was decided for me in consultation with Medea—to start crying. So I did. I was so uncertain of what we could do: They would not let us sleep on the couches in the lobby; we could not leave after curfew. A new man emerged from the office behind the desk and reported that there was one room—"high up," he said, with no heat or water—and this was in bitter cold January. I thought he had meant no *hot* water, but he had said what he meant—no water of any kind.

There was no elevator, not here or anywhere in Kabul. We walked up six flights of hard marble stairs—testament to the fact that the city had once been a thriving, rich metropolis—and down a dark hall—the electricity was out—into the coldest room I had ever known. One of the men brought us a bucket full of cold water for the toilet, which did not flush. Tired, worried, and miserable, I opened the door to our "room" and walked down the hall.

The rooms were all marked with the names of media, and I knocked on the door for CNN. The people who answered knew who I was—one of four visiting Americans who had lost loved ones on

September 11—and that we were a "big story." They were so kind to me, giving me a space heater (to use when the electricity worked), water to drink (with the warning to "never drink tap water here") and some extra blankets. I took these back to our room and we tried to sleep. And we did—sort of.

The next morning we sat at a table in the dining room, drinking tea and watching the ministers, who were slowly returning for the purpose of forming a new government, as they sat at the tables around us and talked. My network interviewers arrived and whisked me away, looking for footage that would add color to their segment. As I marveled at the paper flowers for sale among half-demolished buildings, I was told we were on Chicken Street and was invited to make a purchase while the camera rolled.

I reached for the pouch around my neck holding my passport, return airline tickets, and the $500 I had brought with me. But it was gone. And I panicked. Then I remembered that I had put the pouch under my pillow for safe-keeping the night before—on the top floor of the hotel. My companions calmed me down and sent someone to the hotel to find it. I knew it was lost. I am a New Yorker. An American. I knew that a passport in Afghanistan would be almost priceless. But the man returned with my pouch, and nothing had been taken. And I learned that my luggage, which I had also left behind, was being held for me at the desk.

While everyone has stories about the challenges of traveling in a foreign land, the real story of my trip to Afghanistan is of the people I met.

Everyone we encountered knew about September 11—everyone. In a school for the deaf they had even invented a special sign: Hold up your left hand and move the fingers of your right hand horizontally toward your left palm until they touch. I still get shivers remembering the first time I saw the teacher for deaf kids explain to them who I was. I kept thinking to myself, "How many Americans know anything about Afghanistan?"

We visited the Aschiana Street Children's Center, a humanitarian agency that took children off the streets, fed them a daily meal, and taught them arts and crafts so that they would not have to beg. The children were so beautiful and so sad. But they were also children, and so they laughed, and sang, and gathered around to watch and to hear these strange Americans. After we had been there a few days, we were recognized wherever we went, and the children would call out to us, "Hallo, how are you, we love you."

American forces had dropped many cluster bombs in the military campaign. Each contained 202 "bomblets," which explode separately. De-miners in the area told us that up to thirty percent of the bomblets did not explode on impact—remaining as unexploded ordinance and a danger to the population. At first, they looked like the food packets the U.S. had also dropped from the skies, and those running to get the food would sometimes be maimed or killed. After a while, the colors were changed, but little children—who are not always easily managed by adults—would stray and play in the fields where the bomblets lay ready to explode. A doctor who oversaw both the detonating of unexploded bomblets and the hospital treatment of victims told us that at least ten children a day were so harmed. He described his own children's fear when he returned to his home each evening, and how the noise and flashes of bombs falling all around had terrified them.

I met the brothers of a young man who had recently married for love, a very rare occurrence in a culture where marriages are arranged. He and his new bride were asleep in their bed when a bomb came through the window and killed them both. They told me about their brother: He was an artist and a poet and had married a young woman very much like him.

We sat on a carpet on the floor, drinking tea and eating nuts and raisins brought by their sister, who handed me an embroidered parrot that her brother had made. She said how sorry she was for my brother, and we embraced and cried together. It was only after I left their house that a reporter told me it was almost unheard of for the woman to have stayed in the room and spoken to me. She was that moved by the presence of an American woman who had come all that way to say how sorry she was for the death of their brother.

My trip to Afghanistan changed my life. Never will I be able to turn my eyes or back away from the innocent victims of governments unable to resolve conflict through means other than bombs—bombs that kill innocent people, just like my brother Avrame.

* * *

MUSICAL PASSAGES
by Derrill Bodley

I teach music appreciation in a community college—courses in classical music, popular music, and jazz. Since September 11, music has changed for me. There are certain songs I can't listen to anymore, and other songs for which the meaning or the way I listen to them has changed radically. One of Deora's favorite songs was from the movie *Moulin Rouge,* and I hope I never have to listen to that music again.

In the classical music classes, there are pieces which have symbolic value that never mattered much to me before. When Deora was three or four, we went to see the film version of Bizet's *Carmen* (in French, with subtitles), with Placido Domingo and Julia Megenes-Johnson. I play excerpts of that same video in class every semester, and I am reminded of that special experience with my daughter twenty years ago. My students can't see me crying in the dark . . .

Another time last year in class, I was sharing a story with my students about Beethoven's dedication of the *Eroica* symphony (his third) to Napoleon, a story I have told for many semesters. This time, however, as I began the story, I felt a sudden "catch" in my throat. What was I saying? Beethoven had sympathized with Napoleon's professed egalitarian ideals, and had written a dedication to him on the first page of the musical score. When he heard that Napoleon had crowned himself emperor, he angrily scratched out the dedication, so forcefully that he tore a hole in the paper. I realized that there was something frighteningly similar in this story to our own modern times in America. I barely made it through the story without breaking down and excusing the class.

In the days I visited Afghanistan in January 2002, I was able to play some music with two musicians at the newly restarted Kabul radio station. This "jam session" remains one of the high points of my life. I picked up something in just the few minutes we played together that has permanently affected me musically and personally, and this "something" is invoked in the passages of a song I wrote after September 11, 2002, called "One Year After."

During the trip, I was able to "use" music in two other ways to help bridge the gaps between us and the people there, particularly at a school for orphans and street children that we visited. The night before we left Pakistan for Kabul, I bought a very small Casio keyboard to bring into Afghanistan, with the hopes of doing something with music. When we went to the Aschiana School in Kabul, I brought the little electronic piano, about a foot and a half long, with me.

Outside, in the small schoolyard, some boys were working on calligraphy, which they put on small wooden objects to sell. I said to myself, "This is an opportunity I can't pass up." I asked if I could engage them in a little musical activity. I had prepared about half the words to "This Old Man," a counting song, in Dari, the local version of the Farsi language which is common there. Wakil, the interpreter, explained the other half of the words as I led the boys through singing the first two verses:

> *Mar de peer (This old man),*
> *He played yak (one),*
> *He played knick-knack on my back ("pusht" in Dari),*
> *With a knick-knack paddywack (untranslated),*
> *Give a dog a bone (translated),*
> *Mar de peer khon-a med-a wah (This old man came rolling home).*

Derrill Bodley "knick-knacking" on his back

We did hand motions for *yak, back,* and *knick-knack paddywack.* By the time we got through the second verse (*Du* for *two,* rhymes with *shoe*), everybody was cracking up laughing! It was unforgettable.

Immediately afterwards, we went inside to visit a room full of young girls making paper flowers. The room was little, with a small high window letting the light in to shine on a few faces at a time. I had brought a pocket cassette player with me, along with a tape of songs that had been played at my daughter Deora's memorial services.

One of the songs on the tape was a piece written by my father, J. Russell Bodley, who had been a choir director and composer at the University of the Pacific in my hometown. The music was a piece for a capella choir (unaccompanied voices) called "The Flower Factory." The words were from a poem by the same name from the early 1930s, about four little girls in a cold factory building somewhere in Europe after World War I, making . . . paper flowers. When I saw the young girls in the school making paper flowers in that little room, I knew I had to play that song for them. Wakil explained the song, which sadly describes the poor life these girls were leading, until the ending which lifts up a glorious prayer:

Let them have a long, long playtime,

Lord of toil, Lord of toil—

When toil is done . . . toil is done,

Fill their tiny hands with roses,

Joyous roses . . . joyous roses of the sun.

I had played this song on the organ many times over the years, particularly at memorial and funeral services, because the music contains the movement from sadness to joy that I had loved ever since I heard my father's choirs sing it when I was a child. But the words, which made reference to the Black Hand and terrorist repression in those days, were too specific for any of the choirs I had been associated with over the years. Now, in this case and in this time, the words to the song were once again eerily appropriate.

I had also made several dozen wallet-size copies of a picture of my daughter Deora, taken at her high school graduation. In this picture, she is wearing a white robe and is holding . . . a single rose. On the back of each picture, I had written, *"I am happy to be here in Afghanistan with you,"* in Dari. I passed out the pictures to the girls in the room as Wakil helped me explain that this was my daughter Deora and that she and I hoped they would take advantage of the freedom they now had to attend school (they couldn't during the previous five years under the Taliban) and finish their education. When we left, the teacher was in tears. I felt as if several giant loops of meaning in my life had been completed.

Many people have told me that it was a good thing for me to have music to help me get through what happened September 11 and afterwards. I would have to agree with them. When I was younger, I had grand notions about how one (such as myself) could do great things in the world through music. But Peter Townshend, guitarist with The Who, put it best when he said, "Music can't change the world. Music changes the way one lives in the world." I hope that by sharing music I have helped some of those who have heard it to change, in some positive way, how they live in the world.

Inability to love is the central problem, because that inability masks a certain terror, and that terror is the terror of being touched. And if you can't be touched, you can't be changed. And if you can't be changed, you can't be alive.

—James Baldwin, interview with Jere Real

Chapter Six

As January wore on, decisions had to be made about how and when to launch Peaceful Tomorrows, the group. Tying the launch to the return of the delegation was dismissed as confusing, leaving Potorti to scan his calendar for an appropriate holiday to anchor the event. Valentine's Day emerged as an obvious choice—but could those Valentine hearts promote love between nations as well as people?

He ran the idea by Kathy Kelly, who had a story at hand about St. Valentine. He was a renegade Roman priest at a time when the Emperor was having trouble recruiting soldiers for the military. The reason? They didn't want to leave their families. The solution? The Emperor outlawed marriage. Valentine became known for conducting secret marriages by candlelight. He was eventually discovered and sentenced to death. As he awaited his fate in a prison cell, couples he had married dropped notes through the cell window, expressing their appreciation. He grew close to the jailer's daughter, who would visit him for long, chaste talks. As he departed for his execution, he left her a love note, signed, *"From your Valentine."*

True or not, the idea of "peace notes," stuck into boxes of chocolate, seemed like a nice touch for publicizing the group's web address, while providing the press and the public with much-needed sugar. Colleen Kelly explored chocolate companies that might like to donate their goods, learning along the way that there was a chocolate boycott over child labor practices. Not wanting to stumble unwittingly into controversy, the group dropped the chocolate idea, deciding that the notes could be posted on their website, printed, and used to provoke dicussion among peace groups across the land. Collections like *Barlett's Quotations* provided no shortage of ruminations on the subjects of war and peace.

Barry Amundson began designing a website and a logo, pulled links to press articles that were already being written about the nascent group's members, and incorporated the organization's mission and goals statements along with membership information into a homepage—all while keeping tabs on Campbell's movements in Afghanistan through e-mail and by reading the news like everyone else.

The Afghanistan delegation returned home on January 22, and commanded respectable media coverage at a press conference in which they recounted highlights of their trip and called for the creation of an Afghan Victims Fund.

"I remember having a kind of a 'high-five' moment of enthusiasm with Rita at the press conference," Barry Amundson said, "and then an overwhelming feeling of shame seemed to blanket us, because we both realized that while we were excited by all the TV cameras and attention, and the 'star treatment' that people were giving us, it was our brothers' deaths that caused us to be there. To act in a way that would give honor to their lives, while trying to get into the public eye in order to say things that provoked a sense of reconciliation and contemplation was a very hard thing to do."

The group proposed an Afghan Victims Fund of $20 million—the equivalent of $10,000 each for an estimated two thousand civilian victims (at the time, the U.S. was spending $30 million a day on bombing). But the fund was not just about money, it was also about accountability: promoting the idea that

Kelly Campbell lobbies for Afghan kids at January 2002 press conference.

the decision to bomb also carries with it a price tag in innocent lives, which must be acknowledged; educating the public about the actual effects of war, in human terms as well as in destruction of infrastructure; and protecting American safety by improving its image in the aftermath of war—by being responsible for damages: mental, emotional, physical, and otherwise.

At the time, civilian casualty figures were in dispute, even among those who acknowledged them. Marc Herold, a University of New Hampshire professor, kept a running tally of Afghan civilian deaths, culling information from news agencies, major newspapers (foreign and domestic), and firsthand accounts. His tally was approaching four thousand, but as of this writing, actual casualty figures remain in dispute.

Later that evening, the delegation shared what they'd seen at the Park Slope United Methodist Church, a Brooklyn congregation pastored by Reverend Elizabeth Braddon. Amy Goodman, who served as emcee, petitioned the audience and raised more than $6,000 for the cost of the trip and a private Afghan victims fund that night, demonstrating that Americans continued to care about their counterparts on the other side of the world, even if their politicians remained reticent.

Members of the delegation spent two days in Washington, DC, lobbying Congress and seeing how the Victims Fund would play in the Capitol. The group included Masuda Sultan, an Afghan-American who had supported both Bush and the war but lost nineteen members of her extended family in a U.S. airstrike near Kandahar on October 22, making civilian compensation more than an abstract goal.

They visited two dozen Congressional offices over two days, bringing photos from their trip to illustrate the reality of suffering endured by Afghan families. While support was commonplace, everyone had a different take on how the fund might go through: a presidential act, a Congressional resolution, a State Department fund, a Department of Defense fund . . . ? Ohio Congressman Tony Hall, who had just returned from Afghanistan and had witnessed some of what the delegation had seen, was particularly supportive, suggesting that President Bush would have the power to set up the fund immediately and going so far as to get the President's scheduler on the phone while the delegation was in his office. Congresswoman Carrie Meek of Florida got on board immediately, agreeing to sponsor a resolution and drafting a "dear colleague" letter to circulate through Congress to garner additional support.

"I was kind of shocked, I thought there was going to be so much more resistance to it," Kelly said. "But there was overwhelming support that this was a good idea and was the right thing to do." In fact, support was evident across the political spectrum, from conservatives to liberals, Democrats to Republicans. But the delegation learned another fact about Washington politics: It's easier to be responsive with family members sitting in your office than it is after they leave. Follow-up phone calls to formerly interested parties quickly went unanswered.

As Congresswoman Meek's letter circulated, the delegation

decided that President Bush's inprimatur remained crucial in moving the fund forward. Whenever and wherever they decided to launch their group, they would accompany that announcement with a letter to the President.

* * *

On February 14, a frigid day in New York City, the creation of Peaceful Tomorrows was announced at the UN Church Center, across the street from the United Nations, with speakers including AFSC's New York Regional Director Elizabeth Enloe, Rita Lasar, Colleen Kelly, Phyllis Rodriguez, Kelly Campbell, Ryan and Barry Amundson, and David Potorti, who introduced the group with the Martin Luther King, Jr. quote from which the group took its name. He drew from their mission statement and their goals of seeking effective alternatives to war as a response to the September 11 attacks, and seeking justice, not revenge, for the "crimes against humanity" that occurred that day.

"We believe that our country's single-minded rush to war has been made without proper consideration of the long-term consequences of our safety, security, and freedom of ourselves, our children, our grandchildren, and our counterparts around the world," Potorti said. The need for dialogue was cited as a major concern, reflecting the challenges they had faced in getting their voices heard. "A dialogue between the millions of concerned Americans is a necessary first step in seeking better solutions—solutions that represent the full scope of concerns, held by all Americans," he asserted. "We believe that America is a great nation, with many strengths, and our military strength is just one. We believe that the collective wisdom, skill, and imagination of the American people remains our greatest strength."

The group made this call: "We believe that people from all

walks of life—artists, poets, musicians, teachers . . . everyone—has something to offer as a response to our personal and national tragedies, and we invite everyone to come together and use our group as a rallying point, an opportunity to explore other alternatives to war. In our small way, we would like the formation of Peaceful Tomorrows to be an invitation to start a dialogue and begin a discussion. We believe that peaceful tomorrows begin with what we do today."

Each of the members spoke. "If President Bush were more like my mother," Kelly said, in reference to her mother's willingness to entertain a variety of thoughts and opinions, "the world would be a better place." Campbell spoke about her experiences in Afghanistan and held up a large Valentine's Day heart with a letter to President Bush pasted in the middle, announcing the group's formation along with the Afghan Sister Families Campaign they had launched in conjunction with Global Exchange.

"The families we met with were grateful for the U.S. help in overthrowing the Taliban, know that the U.S. did not intend to harm them, and believe that the United States is their friend," the letter read. "Many of these families also believe that the U.S. will provide some compensation to help them to rebuild their homes, get the medical care they need, and enable them to contribute to the revitalization of a democratic Afghanistan. We would like to turn that belief into a reality." The letter was faxed to the President's scheduling office.

Immediately following the press conference, Campbell and Potorti met with Cora Weiss, president of the Hague Appeal for Peace. She had arranged for the group's travel to New York and would find them their first grant.

* * *

In what would become a frequent practice, the group retired to Lasar's apartment with take-out food and discussed what to do next. There were clear interests among the members: U.S. participation in the International Criminal Court, which recently had been "unsigned" by the Bush Administration; opposition to the death penalty; Afghan reconstruction; military and media reform, education and teach-ins; and on and on. Campbell was quitting her job to work with Peaceful Tomorrows full-time; Potorti, who was already freelancing, would make the group his focus. They would serve as West Coast and East Coast "co-directors." Kelly would later quit her job to become their New York regional coordinator. Ryan Amundson would serve as the group's Midwest coordinator. Barry would take on multiple freelance jobs while serving as the group's website administrator.

It was a curiously hopeful time: In spite of their losses on September 11, they had gained each other, along with the recognition and support of many faith-based and social justice groups. They had gone to Afghanistan and captured the attention of the world. And they had gotten organized—announcing to the press, and to the President, that they intended to continue down the road of what Janet Chisholm had decribed as "transformative nonviolence."

Just how they would achieve their goals remained a question mark. Most of them were siblings of victims and would see no money from 9/11 charities or government disbursements. Their lofty goals were unmatched by specific plans for achieving them. Real sacrifices would have to be made in terms of income and security. But at a time of paralyzing fear, anger, and uncertainty among many Americans, they had a new, liberating focus. September 11th Families for Peaceful Tomorrows was on the move.

Greetings from Malaysia. I found your site from Antiwar.com and I must say that I applaud your efford and I hope God will help you guys.

*

Thank you for your initiative. You are the true Americans. The Bushes should be proud of you but I doubt they are. More greetings from Germany.

*

This is a brave website created by brave people. I hope your message spreads across the United States. If you will permit me one criticism, however, I don't agree that we should promote democracy and human rights in other countries. Such policies are never applied consistently by governments and that in itself will create a great deal of resentment. I think we should simply leave other countries alone. No one has ever hated Americans for not sorting out their problems. America has no international mission other than to give other nations no reason to attack us.

*

Your Muslim brothers and sisters in Canada salute you. May your loved ones rest in peace knowing that you seek peace and mercy between nations in their name.

*

You guys can't be serious? I want peace, but when someone has the intent of killing you, your way of life, then you fight back and defend yourself—to be peaceful in such a case is to invite your own death. Self preservation is the right of all living creatures!

*

Hello from Australia. You have my prayers and my admiration. Perhaps our leaders should think that they now have the chance to create World Peace 1 instead of World War 3.

*

My platoon in Vietnam was wiped out 11 days after I got home. I think of these young men every day and know they are in a better place. I'm not mad at the people of Vietnam, I'm upset with this government, they put us there. I could go on and on about how horrible war is, it proves nothing but screws up people and the environment. Thank you peace and I'm with you. Maybe some day we can get it right.

To fall out of step with one's tribe; to step beyond it into a world that is larger mentally but smaller numerically—if alienation or dissidence is not your habitual or gratifying posture—is a complex, difficult process. It is hard to defy the wisdom of the tribe, the wisdom that values the lives of its members above all others. It will always be unpopular—it will always be deemed unpatriotic—to say that the lives of the members of the other tribe are as valuable as one's own.
—Susan Sontag

Chapter Seven

From the beginning, membership in Peaceful Tomorrows was a sticky subject. They wanted the group to grow, but were keenly sensitive to the fact that everyone was grieving in different ways and on different timetables. Some might be ready to hear their message, and others might not even be able to get out of bed in the morning. The family members did have a particular point of view—some would identify it as a political agenda—which might be misinterpreted or unwelcome. So the goal became for recruits to "self-select" based on agreement with the group's principles.

For the time being, that's exactly what happened. Myrna Bethke, a Methodist minister and mother of two from Freehold, New Jersey, lost her brother, Bill, on the 95th floor of the North Tower, the same floor where Potorti's brother had perished. Bill Bethke was one of a small group of employees that had worked in Marsh & McLennan's Princeton, New Jersey offices but had recently been transferred to the company's lower Manhattan location. Everyone who was transferred had been killed in the attacks.

That Bethke was a minister put her in a unique, and at the same time difficult, position: While ministering to her own grief, she had to minister to the grief of her congregation. She was, however, a strong believer that the church could help give voice to fear and anger, "in ways that are productive," and she even led one of the memorial services at her brother's company.

Bethke heard about Peaceful Tomorrows through a story on the United Methodist News Service, which sent a reporter to cover the group's press conference. She found in it a voice for reconciliation which mirrored her own goals.

"From the beginning, my hopes and prayers were that we would not respond with violence," she said. "I just had such a profound sense of sadness that that was the route we took." When she learned about the group, she considered it an avenue for amplifying her concerns. "I felt a lot of responsibility for speaking out against violence, and thought I'd be heard differently, and maybe more clearly," by joining with others.

Potorti had been invited by the Fellowship of Reconciliation (FOR) to write an essay about Peaceful Tomorrows—entitled, "Choosing Hope Over Experience"—and it was that article, plus a link on their website, that introduced Andrew Rice to the group. Like Bethke, he brought a background in religion to the group, holding a Master of Theological Studies degree from Harvard University Divinity School.

"The fact that there was already a group of family members who were articulating what I was starting to feel really strongly was inspiring, because I didn't have the guts to do it on my own, nor did I know how to do it on my own," Rice said. "I was a little scared that people would think I was crazy. So when I heard about the group, I felt, this is a gift—out of a really bad situation, there were other people, like me, who had taken the initiative to form an organization. We didn't want more suffering to come out of this for other people—that was the moral side of it for me. And the practical side of it was, using bombs and guns to fight terrorism was not going to work anyway. We knew that from day one, out of the empathy we had with others who had lost people to violence. You become part of this larger human family, and you just want to protect people."

Rice was based in New York City, where he worked as a reporter and editor for a BBC television show. But when his brother, David, perished at the Towers, where he worked for the investment firm of Sandler O'Neill, Rice happened to be in Canada, covering the Toronto Film Festival. In the transportation chaos following the attacks, his employer stuck him in a taxi, which drove him from Canada to New York.

Because both Rice and his brother had grown up in Oklahoma City, he decided to move west in the aftermath of September 11 to get closer to his roots and effect positive change in that region of the country. He settled in Houston, where he worked for the Texas Freedom Network, a statewide nonprofit countering the influence of religious extremism in politics. That his life had been turned upside down as a result of religious extremism was an irony not lost on him, and he saw the group as an opportunity.

"I knew we would be listened to on certain issues, more than if we didn't lose someone," he said. "I was starting to see all the scary directions that the Administration was taking us, and I wanted to take advantage of the fact that people were going to put a microphone in front of me, rather than just sit back, be complacent and apathetic, and watch the country go down the tubes."

In Israel, Yitzhak Frankenthal, general manager of The Parents' Circle/Families Forum–Bereaved Families Supporting Reconciliation and Peace—had first reached out to the family members after their Walk for Healing and Peace. Frankenthal had lost his firstborn son, Arik, a soldier in the Israeli military, to the Palestinian terrorist group Hamas in 1994. He founded The Parents' Circle to bring together Israeli and Palestinian parents who had all lost loved ones to the continuing cycle of violence.

Representing 450 families, it reflects the unique religious, political, and social history of the region, yet shares a kinship with
Peaceful Tomorrows both in spirit and in its mission: "We consider it our duty to strive for peace so that other parents' children
live on." Or, as Frankenthal would put it, "My revenge is peace."

In March, although Afghan civilian casualties were only
beginning to be acknowledged by mainstream outlets like the
New York Times, Frankenthal and the members of his group bore
direct witness to their own experiences. In conjunction with the
Palestinian National Movement for Change, Frankenthal
brought 1,050 coffins (250 draped with the flag of Israel and 800
with that of Palestine), representing casualties since the second
Intifada that had begun eighteen months earlier, and laid them
on Dag Hammarskjold Plaza, across the street from the United
Nations. The symbolic act, replicated in Tel Aviv and in
Washington, DC, under the banner, *"Better the Pains of Peace
Than the Agonies of War,"* was the talk of the local New York City
media, with the exception of the newspaper of record. Colleen
Kelly met Frankenthal for the first time and presented two bou-
quets of flowers: to a Palestinian and an Israeli mother.

* * *

As Peaceful Tomorrows was welcoming new allies, the National
Youth and Student Peace Coalition was organizing the April 20
Stop the War Mobilization, the first major antiwar march since
the Gulf War to take place in Washington, DC. It would be a
statement against the Administration's policy of "pre-emption"
that could make Afghanistan the first stop in a series of "wars
without end." Peaceful Tomorrows would join hundreds of other
peace and justice groups, including friends from FOR, Peace
Action, Global Exchange, and the AFSC, for its first public
appearance as a group since its launch in February.

As a rallying call to others to join in the march, Colleen Kelly came across a statement from Albert Bigelow, a World War II Naval Officer and submarine chaser, who in 1958 decided to oppose the testing of nuclear weapons. In a public display of disapproval—and in an effort to draw attention to the practice—he had sailed into the area of the Pacific Ocean used by the United States to conduct H-bomb tests. He wrote an essay about his reasons for going, and later became a member of the American Friends Service Committee.

Bigelow's reasons for going to the test site seemed to parallel the group's attitudes about their own pilgrimage to Washington, and they decided to post his essay on their website. "We believe his singular choice of peaceful protest applies today," they said, "to everyone seeking alternatives to war as a solution to terrorism."

I Am Going Because . . .
by Albert Bigelow

I am going because, as Shakespeare said, "Action is eloquence." Without some direct action, ordinary citizens lack the power any longer to be seen or heard by their government. I am going because it is time to DO something about peace, not just TALK about peace.

I am going because, like all people, in my heart I know that ALL nuclear weapons are monstrous, evil, unworthy of human beings.

I am going because war is no longer a feudal jousting match; it is an unthinkable catastrophe for all people.

I am going because it is now the little children, and most of all, the as-yet-unborn that are the frontline troops. It is my duty to stand between them and this horrible danger.

I am going because it is cowardly and degrading for me to stand by any longer, to consent, and thus to collaborate in atrocities.

I am going because I cannot say that the end justifies the means.

A Quaker, William Penn said, "A good end cannot sanctify evil means; nor must we ever do evil that good may come of it." A Communist, Milovan Djilas, says, "As soon as means which would ensure an end are shown to be evil, the end will show itself to be unrealizable."

I am going because, as Gandhi said, "God sits in the man opposite me, therefore to injure him is to injure God himself."

I am going to witness the deep inward truth we all know, "Force can subdue, but love gains."

I am going because however mistaken, unrighteous, and unrepentent governments may seem, I still believe all people are really good at heart, and that my act will speak to them.

I am going in the hope of helping to change the hearts and minds of men in government. If necessary, I am willing to give my life to help change a policy of fear, force, and destruction to one of trust, kindness, and help.

I am going in order to say, "Quit this race, this arms race. Turn instead to a disarmament race. Stop competing for evil, compete for good."

I am going because I have to—if I am to call myself a human being. When you see something horrible happening, your instinct is to do something about it. You can freeze in fearful apathy or you can even talk yourself into saying that it isn't horrible. I can't do that. I have to act. This is too horrible. We know it. Let's all act.

For many going to the Washington march, it was their first expression of public opposition to the war. It was the first time a number of group members had met each other in person, as well as everyone's introduction Kristina Olsen, who had been speaking out since the death of her sister, Laurie Neira, on American Airlines Flight 11.

A nurse living in Newburyport, Massachusetts, Olsen was also a longtime singer-songwriter. After September 11, she re-released a CD of original music and dedicated a song, "The Art of Being

Kind," written a year earlier, to her sister. While she felt heartened by the President's initial reaction to the terrorist attacks—slow and deliberative, it seemed—she was quickly "shut down" by his decision to bomb Afghanistan, and felt a responsibility to prevent suffering from being perpetuated in her sister's name. She went public with her thoughts on a local radio station, which brought her an invitation to speak and sing at an AFSC peace conference. She picked up a copy of their magazine, *Peace Work,* and noticed an article about the family members' trip to Afghanistan.

"I was so happy—a bittersweet kind of happiness—to find like-minded people," Olsen recalled, "people who said they didn't want others to suffer in the name of justice for their loved ones. Everything that they were quoted as saying, all the things that they were doing, was aligned with how I felt. I knew I had to contact them." After a few initial conversations with members of the group, Olsen flew in to join them for the march.

* * *

April 20 shaped up to be a perfect spring day in Washington, and in many respects the proceedings had an innocent vibe, certainly in comparison with the fall and winter marches that followed. Military action in Afghanistan seemed to be winding down. The drive to Iraq was not yet obvious to the public at large. As the cherry blossoms bloomed, the antiwar movement itself seemed to be popping its head out of the ground and taking a look around. While many longtime activists and groups were on hand, for others there was a sort of novelty about publicly opposing the war; positions had not yet hardened. When veteran activist (and military veteran) Philip Berrigan took the stage, he would see people in the crowd who hadn't even been born at the time of his symbolic burning of selective service records in the sixties, alongside many of his contemporaries.

"The papers have time and time again painted this as college kids out doing the college kid thing," remarked Eva Rupp. "But it wasn't—there were a lot of families there, a lot of religious groups there, a lot of community groups that had come together."

A series of speeches and music took place in the shadow of the Washington Monument. Derrill Bodley, who spoke and sang, said, "Many thousands of people are gathering in Washington to signify, by their presence, the strength and determination of the movement to end the use of war as a supposed tool for peace. I am coming to Washington to lend one more body in support of that movement, and I am very grateful that I have the opportunity to present a message, in words and music, which I hope will provide further strength and determination for all of us."

For the members of Peaceful Tomorrows, it was a chance not only to spend time with stalwarts like Berrigan and Martin Luther King, III, but also to hear the messages of Ron Daniels, of the Center for Constitutional Rights; Erica Smiley, of the Black Radical Congress Youth Caucus; Hussein Ibish, of the Arab-American Anti-Discrimination Committee; Dave Cline, of Veterans for Peace; and others who opened their eyes to the larger context in which their groups were operating.

As the rest of the group stood behind, holding up Peaceful Tomorrows signs and photos of children belonging to their "Afghan Sister Families," Bodley led the house band in a rendition of "Each to Give," a song he wrote in 1971 and now dedicated to his daughter:

The world's made up of those who do,
And those to whom it's done.
But peace would come to every soul
When both of these are as one . . .

Each to give and to receive,
Each to live and to believe . . .

In love.

Got to get the balance right.
Got to move to end the fight.
Then we'll make it through the night,
Into the glorious light.

Each to give and to receive,
Each to live and to believe . . .
Each to give and to receive,
Each to live and to believe . . .

In love.

The crowd, which would grow to 75,000 that day, erupted in applause as he sang the word "love."

The morning rally would merge with another sponsored by International ANSWER, focusing on the need for a Palestinian state, and together they would march through Washington. ANSWER's concerns would dominate the afternoon speeches on the National Mall. Olsen nevertheless brought her guitar and

Barry Amundson, Martin Luther King, III, and Ryan
Amundson at the April 20, 2002 rally in Washington

Marching in Washington, April 20, 2002

managed to secure a spot at the end of the afternoon program. For most of the group and the audience, it was the first time they heard her sing "The Art of Being Kind." It was inspired by the Ella Wheeler Wilcox poem by the same name, which comprises the song's first verse.

One world, one seed,
A little love from time to time . . .
We'll make it grow, a sheltering tree,
And that is all we'll need,
Understanding is the seed,
Love will make it grow
And all the kindness we can show.

One god, one creed,
So many paths that wind and wind,
While just the act of being kind,
Is all we really need.
It's all we really need.
It's all we'll ever need . . .

Olsen's clear soprano voice had a remarkable effect: It seemed to take the edge off the crowd. There was palpable change in the mood. Olsen, it appeared, had achieved her goal of "promoting peace and reminding people of the inherent beauty and goodness of life." In fact, the only arrests that day concerned a group attempting to camp out in a parking garage. Assistant Police Chief Terrance Gainer said, "It's been very peaceful, very orderly."

"I believe the most effective acts of resistance to injustice are sincere displays of sorrow, rather than outrage," said Ryan Amundson. "Peaceful Tomorrows helped bring this tone to the event. Although there was much reason to be angry, displays of outrage were a sure way to turn off fence-sitters. I think our message was something many of the demonstrators there were looking for."

Following the rally, members of the group made another round of visits to Congress to promote interest in the Afghan Victims Fund. They secured the help of Oregon Democrat Earl Blumenhaur, who was willing to put some energy into the initiative—now all they needed was a Republican co-sponsor. Congressman Jim Leach, who represented the Iowa district where Barry and Craig Amundson and Kelly Campbell had grown up, agreed. The congressmen eventually enlisted more than forty of their colleagues in the House of Representatives in support of the fund.

At the State Department, the group learned that their idea was being considered at the highest levels of the Administration, but there was concern that a precedent would be set for compensating other victims of U.S. military action—a precedent that the Administration was unwilling to set. As one State Department official put it, "What will happen when we go to war in Iraq? We'll likely kill tens of thousands of civilians—would we have to compensate *their* families?"

The peace movement in this war is based on sincere desire for a peace, but an absolutely naive view of human nature. Whenever the handles of political power have been turned by naive people disaster has been the result. Naive people fix few problems in human society and one of the hardest problems humanity has ever faced is the problem of war. The peace movement has no positive role to play in this war other than as a therapy cult for people who legitimately fear and loath violence.

*

I am glad we didn't have your attitude during the Revolutionary war, World War I or World War II. You definitely would not be allowed to have this website or the freedom you now enjoy. I guess all those men and women that fought and died so you could have the freedom you have now accomplished nothing. Maybe we should apologize to Germany and Japan for what we did to them in those nasty old wars. Maybe we should pay them compensation for their hardships. As for me, I am glad we have always fought back when we were attacked; it's better than living in slavery!

*

Your search for peace & justice and your empathy for those in Afganistan is praiseworthy. However, I do fear those who trade for portable nuclear weapons and I believe that they would use them on innocents without a moments thought. can we prevent this with peaceful solutions, I am not sure. However I do welcome your organization and your courage to speak out with another point of view. Dissenting opinion is not unpatriotic as some would have us believe. Keep up your search for justice and peaceful tomorrows.

*

I sit here everyday and feel guilt because I have brought two very beautiful children into this very ugly world. There is a light at the end of the tunnel. Isn't the best gift we can give our children today is a peaceful tomorrow?

*

I think what you guys are doing is a very noble cause, but you have a long way to go because just about everybody concerned wants war. Good Luck.

Bring back the fathers!
Bring back the mothers!
Bring back the old people!
Bring back the children!
Bring back the human beings I had contact with!
For as long as there are human beings,
A world of human beings,
Bring back peace,
Unbroken peace.
—Toge Sankichi, *Poems of the Atomic Bomb* (1951)

Chapter Eight

Spring would bring new friendships with a group of atomic bomb survivors, or *hibakusha,* from Japan. They had been children at the time the United States dropped nuclear weapons on their cities, and through fate, luck, or happenstance, survived the carnage, only to live with the effects of the bombings: chronic health problems, years of hatred for the U.S., and finally, a consuming desire to tell their stories—for the people of the world to "never forget." And now, they wanted to meet with members of Peaceful Tomorrows.

The *hibakusha* were members of the Hiroshima Alliance for Nuclear Weapons Abolition (HANWA) and its Nagasaki counterpart (NANWA). Formed on March 20, 2001, HANWA grew out of an effort to unify Hiroshima's peace movement and to facilitate peace actions on a scale larger than any of the groups could accomplish alone. Its stated purpose was to eliminate all nuclear weapons.

The *hibakusha* were troubled by their country's increasing willingness to lend aid and support to American military action—at the time, providing intelligence assistance for the war on Afghanistan—even though the Japanese Constitution's Article 9 forbids direct military participation. And now, the Bush

Meeting the Japanese delegation, April 2002

Administration had announced a new doctrine of first strike, pre-emptive war, without excluding the possibility of the use of nuclear weapons. This made a visit to the U.S. imperative in their minds: to arouse the American public to resist the use of nuclear weapons, and, at the very least, to lay the groundwork for immediate and massive protest in the event that such weapons were used.

HANWA's co-directors, Haruko Moritake and Mitsuo Okamoto, had seen Japanese television coverage of Peaceful Tomorrows' February 14 press conference and had contacted Steve Leeper, a businessman and peace activist, to arrange a meeting with the family members during the delegation's upcoming visit to New York, Washington, DC, and Atlanta. Leeper, who grew up in Tokyo, spoke fluent Japanese, and ran a translation business out of Atlanta, was sympathetic to HANWA's cause and made the connection with Peaceful Tomorrows.

On April 25, Peaceful Tomorrows members Barry Amundson, Kelly Campbell, Colleen Kelly, Rita Lasar, and David Potorti exchanged introductions with members the delegation at their New York hotel. As Japanese television crews and newspaper reporters watched, they told their personal stories of

September 11, and received gifts from the people of Hiroshima and Nagasaki. It was a remarkable meeting across years and generations, one that brought the issues of terrorism and weapons of mass destruction out of the history books and into the present day. Their connection with Peaceful Tomorrows was a way of highlighting those issues for a new generation of Japanese.

"To meet people in their seventies and eighties who had suffered unimaginable loss more than fifty years ago, and to see that their message was still needed today, made me realize that Peaceful Tomorrows was not a short-term commitment but a lifelong journey," Campbell said. "These elderly and wise Japanese visitors were like our own ancestors coming to gently guide us with their wisdom."

World Trade Center viewing platform

Their visit was even more personal for Potorti, whose father had fought in the Pacific in World War II, and had told him about the day the U.S. dropped the bomb on Hiroshima.

"The Marines had 'island hopped' across the South Pacific, and had taken Iwo Jima, with a huge loss of life on both sides," Potorti said. "Their next assignment was a land invasion of Japan, and while they were waiting for orders to move out, someone came running into camp, yelling that the war was over because they had dropped the atomic bomb. But no one knew what the atomic bomb was—they thought it was something out of science fiction. And I realized that today, we *still* don't know what the atomic bomb is—it's an abstraction to us. When I met these people, it all became real. It wasn't an abstraction to them—it was the central moment of their lives, the same way that September 11 has become the central moment of my life. They were still suffering, and today my father is suffering, from the memories of war as well as the death of his son. In the big picture, everybody suffers. Nobody wins."

* * *

Later that day, Peaceful Tomorrows joined their Japanese visitors on the viewing platform at the World Trade Center site. Now cleared of virtually all debris, it resembled little more than a mundane construction site, surrounded by sheets of plywood. But still the crowds came. And for those who had lost family members, merely being in the vicinity remained a deeply affecting experience, bringing them to tears. Reverend T. Kenjitus Nakagaki, head of the New York Buddhist Church, led the group in a moment of silent meditation. As they departed, they passed a temporary mural, affixed to a plywood wall, listing the names of those who had died.

The iron fence surrounding St. Paul's Church, which adjoined the site, was still festooned with hundreds of handmade memorials—signs, cards, banners, and peace cranes. As crowds continued to stream to and from the site, the delegation staked out a space on the sidewalk and, for the benefit of the Japanese television cameras and print reporters, unveiled a banner reading, *"No Terrorism! No War! No Nukes!"* HANWA co-director Haruko Moritake read their "Hiroshima-Nagasaki Message of Condolence."

"We have been deeply moved by the members of the September 11th Families for Peaceful Tomorrows," they wrote. "You rose from the depths of personal despair to announce your opposition to any attempt to use the deaths of your loved ones to justify more killing. You have gone to Afghanistan and extended your hands in friendship to people there who have lost innocent loved ones to bombing raids conducted by your own country. What you have done is a perfect expression of the spirit of Hiroshima and Nagasaki, where so many survivors renounced revenge forever. Instead, because they understood that war and nuclear weapons could rob the entire human family of its future, they have worked ceaselessly against violence and for the world as a whole. We believe that we share with you the firm conviction that we must help the whole human race make a transition from a 'civilization of power' to a 'civilization of love.'"

Family members expressed their appreciation by giving members of the delegation buttons, created by the AFSC, showing the World Trade Center towers as the vertical element of a peace sign. They also distributed small pewter hearts, which originated at the memorial service for Bill Kelly, Jr.

"The theme that ran through every story told about Bill was his kindness," Kelly said. "My family wanted to be able to give people a token from Bill's service, to remind us all to be a little kinder in this world. We handed out eight hundred pewter hearts in the church, not nearly enough for all the attendees. Peaceful Tomorrows recognized the universality of the 'heart,' and borrowed this symbol to use as its own. It brought the Japanese visitors into the new family of Peaceful Tomorrows."

That evening, the delegation traveled to the Buddhist Church of New York for an interfaith prayer offering and spoken testimony by members of Peaceful Tomorrows and their Japanese compatriots. The service took place in front of the statue of Shinan at the church's entrance, the only statue in Hiroshima to survive the bombing. In a remarkable coincidence, the statue had been installed in New York in a ceremony held on September 11, 1955. From a balcony overlooking a crowd of visitors, remarks and welcome were offered by Reverend Nakagaki as well as representatives of three faiths: the Native American Tiokasin Veaux, the Christian Reverend James P. Morton, and the Muslim Imam Muhammad Hatim.

Peaceful Tomorrows accepted a gift of carefully transported oleander tree seedlings—the first vegetation to grow in Hiroshima following the bombing—on behalf of all of the victims of September 11. To the Japanese, the plant symbolizes hope, renewal, and new life. Today, they are alive and well at the Bronx Department of Parks greenhouse. Peaceful Tomorrows hopes they may someday figure into the plans for a World Trade Center Memorial.

Inside the church, the *hibakusha* shared their memories of the day that changed their lives forever. Hidenori Yamaoka recalled being orphaned by the bombing, and having to move to the home of family friends who had children of their own. The

The HANWA delegation and members of Peaceful Tomorrows, April 2002

children, already living in a crowded space, resented his presence and bullied him mercilessly. This painful childhood situation, not of his own making, became the prism through which he remembered the bombing, and was the cause of his long-standing hatred of the United States, which dissipated only after thirty years.

Others spoke of the horror of being one of the few living people in a sea of corpses created by the bombing of Nagasaki, reduced to an animal-like state, eating grass to survive. One survivor, though not killed by the bombing, suffered wounds so excruciatingly painful that she committed suicide only days later. Another's discovery of an abundance of lucky four-leaf clovers in the spring of 1946 seemed to temper her despair; she learned later that their presence was a result of mutation caused by radiation.

At a reception following the event, friendships were cemented and invitations made to visit Japan. The country and its people would prove to be the group's most enthusiastic supporters.

THE ROLE OF INTERFAITH WISDOM IN GRIEVING
by Colleen Kelly

As a child, death seemed fairly remote. My grandfather died when I was twelve—old enough to understand, young enough not to be afraid, and naïve enough to think that was as close as it would get.

I was raised by Roman Catholic parents. I went to Catholic schools, and a Jesuit University. Priests were not uncommon visitors in our home. My faith means a lot to me; more now than it ever did. And although I'm not a prayerful person, the first thing I did on September 11 upon hearing that a plane had hit the World Trade Center was pray.

There was nothing else to do.

My brother Bill didn't work at the Trade Center. He was attending a breakfast conference at Windows on the World. My family had no idea we were personally involved in this tragedy until later that morning. Nothing of Bill has ever been identified, which made our family rethink the rituals of a funeral. We chose then a memorial service. There was no casket, no physical remains of Bill, no burial. We instead hold close his memory, his spirit. We have locks of hair from a five-year-old haircut.

The Catholic rituals of mourning helped greatly: the "wake," the eulogy given by my sisters at the memorial service, being surrounded by relatives and friends in this protective cocoon of sorrow. All this I found comforting and healing. I thought a lot about the Catholic mantra on Ash Wednesday, "Ashes to ashes, dust to dust." For Bill, nothing could be more true.

It was subconscious, and primarily because of my work with Peaceful Tomorrows, but I began to realize how different religious traditions all had something to offer in terms of grief work. This initially became apparent through my good friend Neal, who was raised in the Conservative Jewish tradition. It came at a time when I was first speaking publicly about the loss of Bill. I felt confused, sad, comforted, and at times, intensely pained. Neal told me of a belief within the Jewish tradition which holds that each time you utter the name of your deceased loved one, grace comes into this world. "How beautiful!" I thought. "Whenever I talk about Bill, grace and goodness enters onto our troubled planet." This tenet not only helped me acknowledge Bill's tragic death, but also strengthened my hope that his death not be in vain.

In May of 2002, Peaceful Tomorrows was asked to introduce a panel discussion at the Cathedral of St. John the Divine in New York City. The forum was entitled, "Religion and Reconciliation: Rebuilding from an Interfaith Perspective." One of the speakers was Father Michael Lapsley, an Anglican priest living in South Africa whose hands were blown off when he received a letter bomb because of his work against apartheid. He was the first person to directly look me in the eye and say, "I am so sorry this happened to you." He also told me that I couldn't forgive my brother's murderers (a statement that shocked me!), only Bill could do that. He introduced me to "restorative justice." For example, it's not enough to return the bike you've stolen, perhaps you should buy a new tire for the person you've stolen it from. You have to make amends. Although the concept of restorative justice is neither new to Christianity nor Father Lapsley, it was new to me on this individual level. Another healing salve to apply to my wounded heart.

In the winter of 2002, we were approached by Steve Leeper, an intermediary fluent in both Japanese and English. Several *hibakusha* wanted to come to New York and meet with Peaceful Tomorrows. We readily accepted the idea, and enlisted the help of Reverend Nakagaki of the Buddhist Church of New York. On a sunny day in April 2002, Peaceful Tomorrows accompanied the Japanese delegation to Ground Zero. We had a small ceremony on the platform overlooking what was then still an active recovery site. Buddhists believe in the continuation of life after death. Our chanting and prayers that day were to help the suffering spirits still present at Ground Zero; to release them. Throughout the day, there was something within me that gave permission to let a part of Bill go; a realization that he was okay. It was us here on earth that would have to continue.

We were then graciously permitted to meet with the staff at St. Paul's Chapel, hear of their efforts with the recovery workers, and prayerfully walk through the cemetery separating the chapel and actual Ground Zero site. It was here that we were reminded that Hiroshima was the original "Ground Zero," as that term had first been applied to the epicenter of the atomic blast of August 6, 1945. And here were survivors of that horrific day, perpetrated by my country, to express their deep sorrow for the loss of so many on September 11.

On October 12, 2002, the island of Bali tragically joined the list of terrorist targets. In a place many describe as paradise, over two hundred people were killed at a nightclub. Mid-November, Peaceful Tomorrows was asked to participate in a Balinese Purification and Memorial Service at Ground Zero. The ceremony was simultaneously taking place in most every household on the island of Bali, and was meant to honor the dead of both September 11 and October 12.

The Balinese practice a unique form of Hinduism which holds as its fundamental principle *"tri hita karana"*: a concept of emphasis on the harmony between all things. "Disruption to the *tri hita karana* wrought by disasters of great magnitude requires a special purification ceremony known as *Tawur Agung Pamarisudha Karipubhaya.* This ceremony asks God to forgive the carelessness of humanity that allowed the event to occur; to bless the souls of the victims so that they can find peace; to bless the perpetrators so that they may find enlightenment and repentence; to bless those who have been affected so that they may have peaceful lives; and to bless and maintain the harmonious *tri hita karana.*"

So there we were, at Ground Zero, families of September 11 victims, families affected by the Bali bombing, and scores of friends, supporters, diplomats, and dancers. There were luscious flowers everywhere. After the purification ceremony, we proceeded, accompanied by hauntingly beautiful music, to the edge of the Hudson River. Remembering Father Lapsely, it was my turn to look these parents in the eyes and say how sorry I was for their losses. There was ritual dancing and the burning of incense. Then we took our flowers and threw them into the receding waters of the river. The sun was setting and I remembered how much Bill loved to sail.

My first intimate look at the religious tradition of Islam occurred while I was in Iraq in January 2003. Upon our arrival in Baghdad, we were constantly in the presence of a government minder. Two Iraqi men shared that responsibility during our stay, and both of them left deep and lasting impressions. "Mr. B," as I'll call him, met us at the airport, and had allowed the peace teams meeting our delegation to carry anti-war banners and sing antiwar songs in the airport concourse. He was a devout Muslim, and never without a copy of the Quran in his left hand. What struck me most was his steadfast commitment to the Muslim call to prayer five times a day.

I remember clearly our visit to the al-Amiriyah shelter, where over four hundred Iraqi civilians had been incinerated on the night of February 13, 1991. On the day of our visit, Mr. B was accountable for the actions of our delegation, the Iraqi families meeting us, and the sizable press contingent following this event. The situation was potentially volatile, with Iraqis and Americans who had lost loved ones to violence coming together, compounded by the presence of reporters. Midway through the press conference, I looked over to see Mr. B kneeling in the dirt parking area, facing east and praying. I thought of how rare it was anywhere in this world to see someone placing spiritual concerns before human ones in such a public way.

The Peaceful Tomorrows delegation also visited the family of Jamil Fedah, an Iraqi killed by U.S. bombing in December 2002, in the city of Basra. The women of the family wore the traditional *abaya* and *hijab*, long black robes and head coverings. It was explained to us that their particular Islamic tradition prohibits women in mourning from having any contact with males outside the family for four months. The women in our delegation were therefore allowed into the "mourning room," while the men, including our government minder, were not.

That was the first and only time that we were permitted to be with Iraqis without our minder. We sang, we cried, we attempted to tell stories to each other of our lost loved ones. There was a palpable human connection that transcended all boundaries of national identity, culture, or religion. We stayed for almost an hour, our minder calling several times for us to leave at once. But he never entered the room, even as we repeatedly chose not to heed his call. His respect for the practice of his own religious tradition superceded his job responsibilities—no small thing given that his work was potentially filled with grave consequences.

Religious tradition has been used throughout the ages to promote war, segregation, fear, and hostility. We need only look to the Crusades, the Holocaust, and a host of other examples for proof. Certainly, September 11 can join this infamous list. We know through voice recordings in the cockpit of an airplane that the name of Allah was invoked before these horrendous murders were committed. We also know that in the days after September 11 some national Christian leaders purported that the events of September 11 were a sign of God's displeasure with American society, and that Islam was an "evil religion."

Yet I would suggest that religious traditions are much more commonly invoked to promote peace, healing, and reconciliation. It's the bad stuff that gets all the play. Our challenge, therefore, is to take for ourselves what resonates, brings solace. Be open to healing wherever it may be found.

It's often in the most unexpected places.

Alternitives for violence Huh??You bunch of spoiled,rich, chicken $hit,MORONS.Let em; walk in and kill a few thousand,then set em; down and feed em; a steak,Huh? your a bunch of depraved,lame brains,that if it was up to you,you'd just turn ass and run,and this Great Country known as the U.S.,would cease to exist in a matter of days!All the money we've given these BAS-TARDS over the years and they can just walk in and kill us??Tell you what!Why don't all of you that designed this site,and all the dumb ass's that agree with it,take your stupid ass ideas on over to wherever you think these cure's of your's is gona work and do it personally. Give me film right's,I'll sell ticket's,and make sure your kin that's had enough sense in their head to stay behind ,are taten care of,and a pile of Happy Meals given to the kids,whose daddy's just spread your dumb ass's all over the country side like a jar of Skippy!!It's the GIVE all,crap like you that's killing this Country,and the one's like me that Fought,Bleed,& Died,to keep it Safe & Free.GET THE HELL OUT OF IT ,IF YOU DON'T WHAT TO STAND WITH IT,OR GO CRAW IN A HOLE & SHUT YOUR DAM MOUTH!!!!!!!!!!!!!!!!!!!!

*

As a Vietnam Vet, I can tell you with absolute certainty that it takes far more courage to wage peace than to wage war, particularly when the poor and young do the fighting and dying, while the rich and powerful do the profiting and threatening. The illusion of "win/lose" is just that: an illusion. There is only "win/win" and "lose/lose". Thank you for choosing "win/win"

*

Greetings from across the Sea of Peace! I represent, in a small way, very many in Japan and elsewhere who have hoped that there must be some sane minds like you, beside Barbara Lee, in the U.S. to put a brake on the war-crazed Bush administration. Thank you so much for your love and courage.

*

Thank you for your courageous and compassionate work. I'm a Texan, and I support what you are doing and saying. Surprised? I'm not the only one.

*

There is an old saying that it is as easy to be for Peace in peacetime as it is to be a vegetarian between meals. So what you are doing is tough. We as a nation need to remember that as long as we continue to listen to criticism of our policies with open minds we will continue to learn and progress toward peace and security.

I am always amazed when I go somewhere to talk. They tell me that I give them hope and strength during a scary time, when it is very unpopular, if not dangerous in some cases, to dissent. It's fascinating because I feel that if it were not for local peace groups, then I could not do my work in Peaceful Tomorrows. They are telling me they "need" us to come and speak to them, and I am thinking, "You have no idea how much strength you give me."
—Andrew Rice, Peaceful Tomorrows

Chapter Nine

If "restorative nonviolence" was the group's practice, its greatest expression was through the group's participation in speaking events at schools, churches, rallies, and other events, large and small. Some were organized by existing peace and justice groups. Others grew out of new community organizations born out of a need to discuss current events and come to a better understanding of them. The family members were keynote speakers. They served on panels. They did workshops as a piece of larger gatherings. They got in touch with ordinary people who, in almost every case, exhibited far more intelligence, tolerance, level-headedness, and generosity toward the rest of the world than the official line being reflected in the U.S. media.

The President's simplistic pronouncement, "You are either with us, or with the terrorists," was nowhere reflected in the diversity of opinion and hard questioning taking place among members of the public in towns like San Jose, California; Austin, Texas; Montpelier, Vermont; Providence, Rhode Island; Lyncroft, New Jersey; Cleveland, Ohio; Greensboro, North Carolina; Astoria, Oregon; Kansas City, Missouri; and New Windsor, Maryland. It was like a tale of two cities—or, perhaps, Washington, DC and everywhere else.

For the family members, the welcome and fellowship provided by these communities went a long way toward validating their views and giving them the courage to carry on. They met other September 11 family members who would join the group, like Ruth Rosenblum and Scott Ephriam. They realized that people everywhere were wrestling with the same issues they were. But Colleen Kelly found the most powerful speaking events were the ones she did in her own backyard, for groups like Bronx Action for Justice and Peace, formed by neighbors in the aftermath of September 11.

"People could put me in a context," she said. "They knew me, or saw me at the grocery store, so in a sense my speaking was a kind of 'coming out' about who I was and what had happened, and what my hopes were. When you know someone personally, it gives what they say a real validity. There's a guy I'd see when I picked my kids up at school, a corrections officer at Riker's Island, who said, 'I don't agree with you, but I'm glad that you're doing what you're doing, and I hope it's helpful to you.' When you speak in your own neighborhood, there's a chance for a continuous dialogue, because it may not just stop at the end of your talk."

The speaking events contributed a steady flow of donations to the private Afghan victims fund, and a modest income to continue their work, as did contributions mailed to their post office boxes. And while they were getting to connect with people in parts of the country they had never visited before, the core members of Peaceful Tomorrows spent the rest of their spring and summer at work on a less compelling task: writing grant applications. Small foundation grants were beginning to appear along with the individual donations, and if these weren't enough to pay entire salaries, they could at least cover the cost of stamps and telephone bills.

Separated by great distances, the phone—and particularly

the Internet—were keys to their communication. Weekly "staff meetings" were accomplished by conference calls. "Group retreats" were envisioned someday, but at the time, marches and visits from the groups like the Japanese delegation were the only occasions for Peaceful Tomorrows members to catch up with each other in person.

Still, the need to keep on keeping on—for the group to become a full-time occupation rather than a good-will mission—remained paramount, and was by no means assured. While members of Peaceful Tomorrows were getting ink in print outlets from the *Des Moines Register* to the *South China Morning Post,* from the *San Jose Mercury News* to the *Sydney (Australia) Morning Herald,* a platform like the *Oprah Winfrey Show* had a different cachet and represented a different kind of mainstream legitimacy. So when an *Oprah* producer called to invite members of the Afghanistan delegation on the show, they had reason to believe they'd be making a significant breakthrough in spreading the word about their group, their message, and—since the show would focus on Afghan women—the Afghan Victims Fund. They would show footage from their trip. They would announce the group's web address and talk about its mission. If, as they were told, the show would not be "political," their appearance still made sense.

"A producer said this was not going to be a show where we talk about whether we should have bombed Afghanistan or not," Campbell noted. "She assured me that we *could* talk about Afghan civilian casualties, and so it seemed like it was worth it."

What the caveat really meant, however, would become clear after Bodley, Campbell, Lasar, and Rupp arrived in town on June 27 and camped out in the program's "green room." "We got this really odd speech from a woman telling us they didn't want to get political," Rupp said. "They really tried to stop us from saying anything that would be too controversial. So I think all of us were tongue-tied when we got on the show, because we were so afraid that we were going to be saying the wrong thing. Mentally, they'd kind of intimidated us to the point where I was afraid to say anything."

It got worse. "They told us they never put anybody's website up on the screen, that they only link to them on the *Oprah* website," Campbell said. "And then their lawyers said they couldn't link to our website or even mention Peaceful Tomorrows by name because we weren't incorporated. And this is all happening five minutes before we're supposed to go on." It was already enough for Lasar, who decided then and there to not go on the show.

As the remaining three sat in the front row of the audience, they saw, for the first time, how the show had "packaged" their Afghanistan footage, which was used to introduce them. "It was apparent that it had been edited," Campbell said. "You could watch footage that actually shows people suffering because of U.S. military action, and be misled into thinking it was people suffering because of the Taliban."

The family members looked pained. Oprah asked a single question of each of them. The show moved on to other guests. Afterwards, Campbell made no bones about how angry she was to one of the show's producers. "She said, 'I told you it wasn't going to be political,'" Campbell recalls, "and I said, 'Well, how political is that, to make it look like U.S. bombing is actually the result of the Taliban? That's totally political.'"

Still, the experience identifed a key issue about media appearances. "I got a letter from an American in Japan who had been watching the show with friends," Rupp said. "So lots of people saw the show, and that's good. But the question is whether you, in good conscience, go through the process and swallow your pride and not be psyched out by the producers in order to get your message across. I don't feel like I got my message across at all. After being on several conservative shows, like Fox's *Hannity and Colmes,* the *Oprah* show was the most restraining TV experience I ever had. Everyone else was perfectly fine with me presenting my point of view in whatever way I wanted to. But I guess Oprah's in the entertainment business."

A WEDDING OF SOULS
by Kelly Campbell

Six months after visiting Afghanistan for the first time, I was invited to my first Afghan wedding party—in Queens, New York. Not sure what to expect, I descended into the basement of a lavish Indian restaurant to find a crowd of more than two hundred Afghans—all women and children, except for the groom and close male relatives. The women were stylishly done up, decked in a glittering array of silks, satins, a mixture of Afghan and western party clothes, fine jewelry, and elegantly coiffed hair. The room overflowed with women dancing, eating, talking, and laughing.

My companion, Rita Lasar, and I were among a handful of westerners in the crowd, and we felt severely underdressed. Our beaded, polyester Afghan garments, which seemed embarrassingly posh on the streets of Kabul six months earlier, were now woefully drab and ordinary. We glanced at each other in dismay, but no one else seemed to mind. The parents of the groom gave us their seats at the head table and tempted us with intriguingly spiced desserts, and the women beckoned to us to join the circle of dancers.

Two weeks later, the papers brought news of a different Afghan wedding party—this one in the tiny village of Kakarak, Afghanistan. U.S. forces tragically mistook the Pashtun tradition of firing guns into the air in celebration as hostile fire from Taliban encampments, and dropped seven two-thousand-pound bombs, killing thirty people, mostly women and children, and injuring forty more.

Afghan wedding party, Queens, New York

The *New York Times* ran a photograph of Palako, a six-year-old girl who was the only one in her family to survive the wedding party attack. In the photo she is lying bandaged on the hospital bed, still wearing her sequined party dress. Her image brought me back instantly to the basement party, where she would have fit right in among the crowd of children blowing kazoos in celebration, dancing with an aunt, or sitting on the stairs eating wedding cake with her friends.

But Palako was not at the wedding party in New York. Instead, she joins the heartbreaking ranks of less fortunate children I met while visiting Afghanistan in the immediate aftermath of the U.S. bombing campaign in January 2002. Orphaned. Traumatized. Terrified of the death that fell from the sky when U.S. bombs dropped on their homes. And for Palako, it all happened at a wedding party.

Palako's photo also brought me back to September 8, 2001. I was at another wedding party—my brother's. It was an Irish-Catholic affair in Chicago, and I danced blissfully in my floor-length mint-green bridesmaid's dress. Three days later, the unexpected death of Craig Amundson at the Pentagon, on September 11, brought another set of family members together for a less joyful gathering.

Nine months after Craig's death, I danced again for the first time at the Afghan party in New York, laughing, stumbling, colliding, trying to learn the subtle rhythm of the Afghan women's circular dance. And I realized how human families are created when worlds collide in joy, friendship, sorrow, and heartbreak.

In October 2001, the Afghan groom in Queens lost nineteen members of his extended family in a U.S. bombing raid on a village outside of Khandahar—twenty people, if you count a pregnant woman's unborn child. The raid was part of America's new war on terrorism, undertaken in response to the tragedy that touched my family so deeply. Survivors of the village bombing in the grooms' family talk of mothers clutching their children as they fled their homes in the dark confusion of night as gunships fired upon them. Children who were there pull aside their clothing to reveal bullet wounds with scars barely healing. I know this story not from the news media, but from the groom's sister, Masuda Sultan, who visited her family in Khandahar shortly before I went to Kabul.

The American government has issued no explanation, acknowledgment, or apology for the attack on Masuda's family, or the U.S. bombs that destroyed homes, buried children under rubble, and devastated more than a dozen families I met in Kabul, or the countless other innocents who suffered in our government's clumsy attempt to "respond" to the death of Craig and the other victims of September 11.

In Kabul, I met families with the familiar look of shock and pain that my family members wore after Craig's death. An Afghan mother cried as she told us about her five-year-old daughter, who had been the center of her world, being crushed in the rubble as an errant U.S. bomb hit their home. Seared into my brain are the images of trembling children who witnessed the bombing of their neighborhoods. Forever in my heart is the story of Arifah, whose husband and seven other members of her family were killed when a U.S. bomb destroyed their home.

We met Afghans who told us, the families of September 11 victims, "I am so sorry for your loss; your pain is our pain." Many of these people were already suffering before our military actions destroyed their homes and killed their families. How incredible that they could feel compassion for Americans. How important that we build on this mutual sympathy. How essential that we cry together, hold each other's pain in each of our hearts, and find ways to heal this global heartbreak as a human family.

But how does this healing occur? How do we get beyond the false divisions that separate "us" from "them"? How do we reach beyond those who have felt the pain of violence to those who have only watched a sanitized version of it on television? How do we reach the hearts of teenage American boys—the toughest audience I have yet encountered—who assert knowledgably (or, repeating what they have seen on television) that this was the most precise bombing campaign in the history of the world, that some civilian casualties are to be expected, and that Afghan lives are somehow worth less than American lives?

Back in New York, Rita and I stood drinking tea as Masuda and her sisters led a line of young women, now changed into brightly colored dresses with clanging coins, snaking through the crowd in an ancient tribal dance. Marveling at the bittersweet stroke of fate that brought us—a 70-year-old Jewish grandmother from New York and a 30-year-old Californian—we found ourselves the sole westerners left at this Afghan wedding party. It was sorrow and chance that drew Rita, Masuda, and me together: the loss of Craig Amundson and Abe Zelmanowitz on September 11, and the loss of Masuda's relatives in the bombing raid. The responsibility to help the families we met in Afghanistan who have been devastated not only by twenty-three years of war, but also by our own government's actions, binds us in an unbreakable sisterhood.

We cannot erase the horror that descended upon that joyous wedding gathering in Kakarak, any more than we can bring back the dead from September 11. But just as the world reached out to our families, we Americans can reach out to those who were affected in Afghanistan with friendship and compassion, and acknowledge that their pain is our pain. And that their destiny is forever linked to our destiny.

It is only when we recognize and begin to act on the knowledge that we are truly one human family, that we can bring honor to those who died while the human family was still learning this lesson.

May your organization, and others promoting peaceful solutions to strife, eventually link together in a world-wide call for discussion instead of rhetoric, compassion instead of aggression, and understanding instead of retribution. Our individual voices and actions are lovely instruments, but an orchestra is more likely to be heard.

*

I wonder if Osama would have a change of heart after reading some of these love-filled responses here. Would he put down his gun and Small Pox-laden bombs he is building for NYC? No, he'll probably look up your addresses and focus his attacks on you, because you are the weak, the uneducated, the ones who will not fight back. Do any of you get it yet? There are people who do not listen to reason. They are the ones we use force against. And the force is mighty.

*

Do you think that this organizations right to publish this website is protected by the First Ammendement?? Guess what? It's not . . . It's protected by such men as my uncle who was killed in WWII, so that we're not saluting Hitler today. Likewise, any women out there? How would you like to shut up, and not express thoughts? Don't ask for whom the bell tolls, it tolls for thee.

*

I am a wartime soldier. To fight alongside America, and dare I say, Russian soldiers against an evil and cruel enemy was a proud and honourable duty. To rain down bombs on a ruined nation without any defences is a coward's war.

*

here in Australia, it all seems so distant and yet so close. Our media coverage is somewhat skewed and i get so upset by all the hate and supposed "justice". I am very pleased to hear of an organisation that promotes peace and love in a troubled world. And proud that the affected families are taking a peaceful stance. Thank you.

*

I think that this war is a stupid thing to be doing . . . why punish all the kids and civilians that didnt do anything?

We have learned that we cannot live alone, at peace;
that our own well-being is dependent on the
well-being of other nations, far away.
—President Franklin Roosevelt

Chapter Ten

As summer 2002 approached, delegations were traveling to and from Afghanistan on a regular basis to assess the humanitarian situation there. Peaceful Tomorrows viewed the opportunity to join one of those delegations as a chance to revisit families they had met in January and to draw attention to the ongoing Afghan Victims Fund.

Efforts to build support for the fund among the public and the media had been relatively successful—an editorial board meeting with the *San Jose Mercury News* and the *Sacramento Bee* brought favorable editorials, and, finally, a *New York Times* editorial in favor of the fund made the group feel like the idea was gaining momentum. Global Exchange commissioned a Zogby International poll in June which revealed that sixty-nine percent of Americans supported the U.S. government providing humanitarian assistance to Afghan civilians.

The June 16–29 interfaith delegation, sponsored once again by Global Exchange, aimed at identifying ways in which the faith community could support humanitarian projects in Kabul, including the rebuilding of schools, clinics, and mosques destroyed during the U.S.-led bombing campaign. Participants included Bishop Thomas Gumbleton of Detroit, Bishop C. Joseph Sprague of Chicago, Dave Robinson, national coordinator of Pax Christi USA, and Peaceful Tomorrows' Myrna Bethke and Kristina Olsen.

Both of the family members raised travel funds from their

Kristina, Arifah, and Myrna in Afghanistan, June 2002

communities—Olsen, from speaking and singing, and Bethke, from her New Jersey congregation. The *New York Times,* in a May 26, 2002 article by Dean E. Murphy, entitled, *"Beyond Justice: The Eternal Struggle to Forgive,"* mentioned Peaceful Tomorrows for the first time—no small validation for the group—as it remarked upon Bethke's planned Kabul journey after losing her brother on September 11:

> She says she has forgiven his killers, but makes a distinction between retaliation, which she is against, and consequences, which she is for. She is going to Kabul in part to help remind herself that the people there have names and faces—making it harder to want to retaliate against them.
>
> Forgiving her brother's killers, she says, released her from a tremendous burden. "You are free to live again," Ms. Bethke said.

Like the January delegation, they visited schools, hospitals, aid agency offices, and camps for displaced people. They met Afghan women who had lost family to U.S. bombs—including Arifah, the subject of the impromptu press conference in January—and held a memorial service for Afghan families at a Kabul mental health hospital. They visited an orphanage for girls that had been closed by the Taliban and was now open again. And they encountered the same unexpected mix of grief for lost loved ones and gratitude for being freed from the repressive regime.

Olsen acknowledged that her belief that lasting peace could be achieved only by nonviolent means—education, aid, and negotiation—was tempered by firsthand observations of how the forced removal of the Taliban had brought stability and hope to people. "I have always felt, and will always feel, that bombing Afghanistan was wrong," she said, "but it made me question myself and forced me to think about practical solutions and alternatives to war. Bombing one of the poorest countries in the world wasn't the answer."

CHOOSE LIFE
by Myrna Bethke,
based on a sermon delivered following 9/11

See, I have set before you today life and prosperity, death and adversity. If you obey the commandments of the Lord your God that I am commanding you today, by loving the Lord your God, walking in His ways, and observing His commandments, decrees, and ordinances, then you shall live and become numerous, and the Lord your God will bless you in the land that you are entering to possess. But if your heart turns away and you do not hear, but are led astray to bow down to other gods and serve them, I declare to you today that you shall perish; you shall not live long in the land that you are crossing the Jordan to enter and possess. I call heaven and earth to witness against you today that I have set before you life and death, blessings and curses. Choose life so that you and your descendants may live, loving the Lord your God, obeying Him, and holding fast to Him; for that means life to you and length of days, so that you may live in the land that the Lord swore to give your ancestors, to Abraham, to Isaac, and to Jacob.

—Deuteronomy 30:15-20

I recently came across a quote from the social historian Howard Zinn on the wall of the women's room at a Quaker retreat I attended (Quakers having different bathroom graffiti than most!). You can imagine how silly I felt to take my notebook and pen and sit on the bathroom floor to copy this:

> To be hopeful in bad times is not just foolishly romantic. It is based on the fact that human history is a history not only of cruelty but also of compassion, sacrifice, courage, kindness. What we choose to emphasize in this complex history will determine our lives. If we see only the worst, it destroys our capacity to do something. If we remember those times and places, and there are so many—where people have behaved magnificently, this gives us the energy to act, and at least the possibility of sending this spinning top of a world in a different direction. And if we do act, in however a small way, we don't have to wait for some grand utopian future. The future is an infinite succession of presents, and to live now as we think human beings should live in defiance of all that is bad around us, is itself a marvelous victory. (From *You Can't Be Neutral on a Moving Train*)

Those two readings set the context for me in responding to the terror of September 11, and now in responding to the questions of what we do in Iraq and other places of the world when conflict arises. In the midst of threat and fear, chaos and terror, it is easy to lose perspective. I had the privilege of walking down the ramp into Ground Zero in January. The ramp is much longer and steeper than it appears on TV. What I also realized was that it is difficult to keep a sense of perspective about where you are. On the one hand the site is huge, so you feel dwarfed when standing on Ground Zero. At the same time it is hard to imagine the site is big enough to have contained the buildings that it did, particularly two 110-story skyscrapers. I found the experience disorienting, and a reminder of how easy it is to lose perspective when events of the world swirl out of control; how many times life seems both too big and too small all at the same time. In many ways I see that happening now as we react rather than respond to events in the world.

I write this as both a United Methodist Pastor and a September 11 family member. Along with all of you I watched in numbing horror the unfolding events of that day as plane after plane crashed, wondering where it would end. I did not know in the first few moments as I watched, just how personal this tragedy was to become. My family joined all of those you saw on the news . . . posting pictures of my brother on the streets of New York City, visiting the area hospitals . . . posting e-mail messages with his picture. It became clear after about a day of checking the e-mail messages that everyone was looking for employees of Cantor Fitzgerald and employees of Marsh & McLennan, where my brother worked. No one was hearing from those who worked on the ten floors occupied by these two companies in Tower One. We knew that if my brother had been in his office, he was in that area. It was on Thursday that we received confirmation that my youngest brother, Bill, was on the 95th floor of the first tower hit—in the direct path of Flight 11. The only "official" confirmation of his death to this day is his silence. In the days to come there was no way to imagine that this tragedy would lead me to travel to Afghanistan as part of an interfaith peace delegation. Even now I shake my head at how my life has changed. In the first days all I knew was that this was a very public grieving, and that there were responses that I needed to make as a United Methodist Pastor and as a sister experiencing great loss.

It is from those two places that I write, as family member and pastor. I want to offer two different strands of life after September 11 that for me have become inseparably woven together. The first is a theological reflection on the church's response, mine in particular, to the events. The second is my own personal journey as I found myself taking on a new identity: a family member. Even today that is all you have to say, and there is instant knowledge that you lost someone on September 11.

As Tuesday, September 11 hit us, I found myself deeply thankful for the foundations that the church offered. In the context of the church I found it possible to respond to the horrors of the day rather that reacting to them. My congregation is about an hour from New York City. We have a fair number of people who commute to the city for work. And so, on that evening when we gathered for worship, we worshiped with people who had managed the five- or six-hour journey out of the city, we worshiped with members who still had family missing. We gathered mostly in a profound sense of shock and anger. Worship provided a safe place for those feelings. A safe context in which to lift up the terrible sense of violation we felt and place them in the context of a loving God who was big enough to handle them.

In that safety we raged by reading Psalm 137 in its entirety, which ends with this horrible wish: *"Happy shall they be who pay you back what you have done to us! Happy shall they be who take your little ones and dash them against the rock!"* Recently I spoke at a Shiite mosque and shared these words from Hebrew Scriptures, telling the group that the Bible had just as many, if not more, difficult texts than the Quran, and that my understanding was that in the Bible and the Quran these were texts of lament, and not calls to action. We knew Rachel's pain as recorded in Jeremiah: *"A voice is heard in Ramah, lamentation and bitter weeping. Rachel is weeping for her children; she refuses to be comforted for her children, because they are no more."*

There was no sense we needed to "fix" anything that night, nor to make sense of what had happened. Rather, our spiritual task for the night was to give voice to our raw emotions in a safe place, in a safe and appropriate way. On Wednesday we gathered again for worship and this time offered a service of healing. Yet even in the midst of that there was no sense we needed to rush anywhere to make sense of these days. Our worship was more an affirmation of hope for the future. We continued to keep the doors to the church physically open for the week as members of the community needed to have a place of sanctuary. We later heard how important those open doors were for the community. One can never prepare for such events, but we can know what to do when they occur. For me, this is the value of a spiritual place to work from.

On Sunday, as we talked about bringing about a new world in which such tragedies were no longer possible because we had learned to bring about a world where all had dignity and respect, I remember saying this: "We will either rise or sink to this occasion." Those words have stuck with me in my journey since.

When, on October 7 of 2001, the bombs started dropping on Afghanistan, I found myself profoundly saddened that this was the course our country had chosen in response to the terrorists' actions. Ironically, that was my brother's birthday. I know there are some who would find that a fitting vindication for his death. But there is no part of me that finds returning violence for violence a lasting solution, not even to the horrors of September 11. War is not a vindication for the lives of those family members we lost. After the bombings began, I found myself longing to "do something," but had no idea what shape that would take. That something became clear when I heard of a group of family members called September 11th Families for Peaceful Tomorrows. The issues of forgiveness, restorative justice, and reconciliation are lived out for me in this group and other similar groups. Being a part of this group makes a statement about what will define and shape my life—the actions of the terrorists or the love of God.

In June of 2002 I was invited to go to Afghanistan. The scripture text that I began with are among the last words attributed to Moses as he faced his death, and the people of Israel were about to cross the Jordan River to the promised land. They are also the words of scripture that came to me most strongly during my time in Afghanistan. *"I call heaven and earth to witness against you today that I have set before you life and death, blessings and curses . . . choose life."* The first impression of Afghanistan is of flying into Kabul's airport at an impossibly steep angle to meet the ground. And then taxiing down the runway of a heavily mined airport that is littered with the rusting hulks of tanks and trucks and bombed pieces of airplanes chronicling the decades of war in the country—a litany of the many times death has been chosen over life in this country, both from within and without Afghanistan.

Very early in the trip we visited Halo Trust, a de-mining organization. We traveled with the head of the group to a de-mining camp in Bagram where we watched the de-miners at work, a tedious, very dangerous job. It was there we learned the meaning of the white and red rocks we had seen lining pathways and roads. It marked the places that were free of mines. The white side of the pathway was clear . . . the red side marked where the land had not yet been de-mined. I wondered about the people who had to live in villages that were marked out by those pathways, how they coped with the daily reality that a misstep could mean the difference between life and death. I wondered what the children running through those pathways felt, if they knew how dangerous their play could be. The line between life and death, blessing and curse, was very thin.

The image of the red and white rock stayed with me as a symbol of the choices we make between blessing and curse, life and death, and how fine that line can be. Every day we are faced with such choices and probably don't even know we are. We walk the pathways between red and white rocks that have become invisible to us. My time in Afghanistan made me realize how much more carefully we need to live our lives, becoming aware of the choices we make, for each one of them is between blessing and curse, life and death. And attention to the smallest of choices we make, the tiniest of details, matters!

I was reminded of this in a humorous way when reading a book called *An Unexpected Light,* by Jason Elliott, about his travels through Afghanistan. The writer talked of learning the nuances of Dari. In Dari, one of the two official languages of Afghanistan, ask someone, *"Chotor (chetur) hasti,"* and you have asked them, "How are you?" But change one letter and say *shotor* and you have called them a camel! The details matter in the most mundane choices that we make. The details show the world that we choose life over death, blessing over curse. The

Afghan people are known for the depth of their hospitality. Everywhere we went, we were greeted with the utmost respect and hospitality. Even when we visited the homes, or what was left of them, of those who had been affected by U.S. bombing raids, we were greeted in that manner. Even when people did not have enough to offer, we were offered tea, and in most cases lunch. It was always hospitality over enmity. The detail and care of their hospitality was a lesson to me in choosing life and blessing. I wonder how different our lives would be if we took the choice of hospitality seriously at all times and places.

My trip also reinforced my understanding of how intimately we are bound with the global community. What affects one affects us all. In the 1980s, when a volcano erupted in the South Pacific, our weather here was changed. A fire in Quebec last summer filled our skies with haze. The Chinese have a saying that the brush of a butterfly's wings changes the world. The interweaving of our lives was demonstrated by some vivid parallels I witnessed in Kabul. One of the enduring images of September 11 is the picture of the rescue workers raising the American flag over the still-smoldering wreckage of the World Trade Center. That picture became a symbol of hope. All over the roadside graves and in the cemeteries of Afghanistan are green flags raised on the graves of those who have died in the wars of the past twenty-five years. They, too, have become symbols of working toward a time when there is peace in the country.

Another parallel for me was the rubble of much of Kabul. I have a tiny piece of the rubble of the World Trade Center carefully chipped from the memorial to my brother in his home town. Next to it is now a piece of marble that was taken from the rubble of one of the royal palaces in Kabul, its grandeur reduced to a shell of concrete strewn with shattered glass and broken dreams—for me, a reminder of how important it is to work for life and blessing so that such events become the exception rather than the norm of life.

The third vivid parallel was one of life. Many babies have been born into families affected by the loss of September 11. Their lives have been celebrated in a special way. I found the same in Afghanistan. There is a woman named Royla whose two children were killed during a U.S. bombing raid. Royla was pregnant at the time, and has since given birth to Ali, named after her son who died. The flags, the rubble, the new life, all reminders of how crucial it is to make the choices that will lead to blessing and life in the global community.

We were given a lesson in our common humanity by the elder of the Internally Displaced Persons camp we visited. One of our group members asked what the camp needed. With great dignity that man answered: "What do you think I am, a cow? I am a human being like you. I need the same things . . . food, water, housing, education, medical care. All the things you need and have . . . I need them as well." Indeed, the things that bring life and blessing are what we all need!

As I have reflected on my incredible journey over the past year and a half, I find myself asking these questions: What choices are we making that will lead to life? What defines us? I am often asked how September 11 changed me. While there are some obvious ways that I have been changed, at one level I have to respond that it did not change me. September 11 did not change the character of God, and as a person of faith, the foundations of my faith are still the same. The foundation promises that I know are still there. It is from that foundation that I choose to live my life.

Signs of choosing life were evident at every turn in Afghanistan. It is fragile, however, as life is everywhere. We found that while no one was happy that we had bombed the country in our effort to destroy the Taliban, it was now a done deal. The question became, now what? We were told to work for the expansion of the International Security Assistance Force (ISAF). Over and over again we were urged to come back to the U.S. and tell the government not to abandon the country this time.

One of the most poignant moments for me last year came in calling my father a few weeks after September 11. He asked if I could call him back because the New Jersey State Police had just arrived to take a DNA sample from him in hopes of being able to identify my brother. I can remember feeling horrible that he would have to do that—no parent should have to do such things. That moment became joined with another for me, from Afghanistan. A young girl shared her story about the night that the bombs fell on her house. She had to speak because she was the only one left. Again, I felt horrible that she, at the age of eight, was standing before us, listing the family members who had been killed. No child should have to do that!

Knowing firsthand the grief of September 11 has led to my commitment to working toward peaceful resolutions to the world's differences. We work for a world in which parents are not called on to identify the remains of their children, and children do not have to speak for the loss of their family. My hope is that we all find ways to reflect on our decisions and actions and bring this new world into reality.

*I came to Japan, having gone from one Ground Zero—
lower Manhattan, in New York City—to a second Ground
Zero—Afghanistan, and I am now on the original
Ground Zero. So I suppose you might say that my perspective changed. I was adding atrocities to my consciousness,
which in turn makes me more dedicated to pleading with
my fellow humans to start thinking truly about nonviolent
responses to provocations. We cannot expect to continue
along a path that inevitably leads to self-annihilation.*
            —Rita Lasar, Peaceful Tomorrows

Chapter Eleven

Peaceful Tomorrows had struck such a chord with Japanese
viewers that the New Japan Women's Association, known as the
Shinfujin, in cooperation with the Women's Peace Fund, invited
Rita Lasar to give the keynote speeches at two major international
events taking place there. In sheer numbers alone, it would be
difficult for Americans to fathom their global impact and importance. The World Conference Against Atomic and Hydrogen
Bombs, August 2–9, 2002, attracted ten thousand participants
and one hundred delegates from nations around the world. At
the Japan Mother's Congress held just before, ten thousand
women gathered to discuss issues ranging from child-rearing,
education, working conditions, and global issues—like nuclear
abolition—pertaining to war and peace. The Mother's Congress
originated in 1955, and over the course of two days offered fifty
workshops for participants.

While there was a certain formality to Lasar's keynote
speeches—they had to be written well in advance of her arrival,
to allow time for preparation of translations—she also looked
forward to a more relaxed occasion: a reunion with the
hibakusha delegation that had visited New York in April. But in
fact, much like her visit to Afghanistan, the Japanese press pro-

voked a tsunami of coverage that quickly became overwhelming. Reporters were fascinated to learn of the presence of Americans who fundamentally disgreed with the militaristic focus of the "war on terrorism." She found herself speaking three or four times a day to various groups in every city she visited: Fukuoka, Kyoto, and Hiroshima.

"I am honored to be able to visit your country, the country that suffered the most horrendous violence the world has ever perpetrated," Lasar said in her address to the Conference on Atomic and Hydrogen Bombs. "The model Japan exhibits to humanity, of seeking peace where others seek its opposite, is an inspiration to me. I hope, by my visit, to show that there are people in the U.S. who are not inherently vengeance-seekers, who are looking for peaceful ways to counteract the violent act."

Oddly, her biggest concern had been what she should bring as gifts or tokens for her Japanese hosts, who were so generous in their affections during visits and interviews in the United States. She brought pewter hearts, AFSC peace buttons, War Resisters League pins—a tiny gun broken in half—and even went to a flea market and found World Trade Center keychains. "I thought, this is so kitsch," Lasar said, "but they wanted images of the World Trade Center, which they didn't have in Japan."

After she arrived, she was moved to make more personal exchanges. "Moritake-san took me for a personal tour of the Peace Park in Hiroshima, and we spent two hours there," she said. "I was wearing a beautiul Mexican necklace that had been given to me as a gift—it was meaningful to me—and I took it off and put it around her neck, and said, 'I want you to have this.' She cried. I had lunch with one of the women responsible for the trip, and I was wearing a jade necklace that my mother had given me. I put it around her neck, and she gave me her ring. I gave them things I had not planned to give them, but things that I felt compelled to give them in the moment. I wanted them to have something that was part of my whole life, not just my life since September 11."

Despite the obvious differences between Afghanistan, the United States, and Japan, Lasar saw a common thread of suffering among them all in the wake of September 11. Behind the facade of modern-day Hiroshima, she detected a subtle sadness. "Its newness and beauty is actually ugly," she observed matter-of-factly, "because the entire city was destroyed and had to be rebuilt."

Rita joins a march through Fukuoka, following the Mother's Congress, August 2002

After witnessing the destruction of the Twin Towers, and contemplating the devastation in Afghanistan, she discovered that she had even more to learn about human suffering during a visit to the Peace Museum at the original Ground Zero in Hiroshima. Three images she saw there remain seared into her heart. An urn, partly obliterated on one side and completely whole on the other, demonstrated the force of the wind, generated by the nuclear blast, that sliced through the object like a laser. A negative image of a person on a staircase was indelibly etched into the wall, while the person who cast the "shadow" had been obliterated. A diorama, depicting a mother and child in flames, skin beginning to peel off, but alive and running toward a river for relief, captured the horror of the moment. "I do not think that anything compares to August 6, 1945," Lasar said. "It is the most obscene, inhumane event in the history of mankind."

Still, her presumptions would continue to be tested. "There were a couple of people who told me that dropping the bomb was the best thing that ever happened to Japan—that if it hadn't happened, it would still be an imperialist country," she said. "And these were Japanese 'peaceniks.' I don't know how to deal with the idea that I would be glad my brother died because it changed my country."

POWER OF GESTURE
by David Potorti

Not one of us knows what effect we may be having or what we may be giving to other persons. It is hidden from us and shall remain so. Often we are permitted to see a very little portion of this, so that we may not become discouraged. Power works in mysterious ways.

—Albert Schweitzer

On Fourth of July weekend, 2002, I was on a plane going from North Carolina to Baltimore, Maryland to join Rita Lasar for a speaking event: We had been invited to address the first joint convention of the Islamic Circle of North America and the Muslim American Society. The theme of the gathering was "Challenges, Hopes, and Responsibilities," and all three were on my mind as I flew.

After a while, I noticed two African-American kids, probably teenagers, sitting on the plane and flipping through thick guidebooks, the kind tourists take with them on vacation—only these were labeled, *"Afghanistan."* A glance at their haircuts and physical condition told me that they were servicemen in civilian clothes, and even though they were horsing around like they were going on vacation, it was pretty clear that Afghanistan was their final destination.

The flight crew noticed, too, and the pilot came on the intercom with an announcement. "I understand we have some servicemen on board today," he said "We want you to know that all of America supports what you're doing." It was a gesture of solidarity—a slightly presumptuous one, to be sure—and I know it was appreciated. The stewardesses offered them free drinks. "We hope you come back and see us real soon," they said.

How odd it was to be sitting there, the brother of a September 11 victim, disagreeing with our country's decision to bomb Afghanistan, and about to mingle with ten thousand Muslim-Americans to discuss alternatives to war, all on Independence Day weekend! What would that plane full of people think of me? Would the pilot suggest that "all of America supports what I'm doing" because I want to connect with Muslims? Was I wrong to feel just as patriotic as those servicemen—and just as brave?

It wasn't until an interfaith dinner marking the start of the convention that I got my solidarity statement. I had told the story of my brother's loss at the World Trade Center and the creation of September 11th Families for Peaceful Tomorrows when Shaker Elsayed, secretary general of the Muslim American Society, said, "David, your brother was our brother, and we pray for his soul."

Praying, at the gathering, was no small thing: Thousands of observant Muslims gathered in a huge prayer room at the appointed hours, demonstrating that even the happy chaos of a convention was not going to distract them from practicing their faith. Somehow his remark remains one of the most moving things that anyone has ever said to me, and at the same time, one of the simplest gestures of unity and goodwill. They were just words, but I remember them, and in remembering them I recall countless other words and gestures that have come in particular places and at particular times when I needed them the most.

Among them were the words my brother, Jim, shared when I had been unceremoniously dumped by a girlfriend and, broke and alone, found myself moving into a ratty, six-story walk-up apartment in New York. "It's only temporary," he said. And for the better part of a year, I told myself that it was only temporary. And because I told myself it was only temporary, it was. That's what I needed to hear.

Words and gestures are powerful things, and I wonder why we fail to recognize their power. A look, a touch, a tone of voice—these little things sustain us, day by day. And they are the things we carry with us, across days, weeks, and years.

I remember, as a kid of three, bouncing up and down as I watched my father walk down the length of our front porch, home at three in the afternoon from the factory job he held for thirty years. He would be wearing a short-sleeved shirt with a T-shirt beneath it, drab olive pants, and carrying a gray dome-top lunchpail. I would squeal with joy at his arrival, and he would tousle my hair with his big hand as he made his way toward the kitchen. Forty years later I can still feel his hand on my head as if he had just put it there, the same way I put my hand on the head of my son, who is today three years old.

The power of gestures to span lifetimes provides an answer to a question I frequently ask myself about the work of Peaceful Tomorrows: Does it matter? Does an act of solidarity with a Muslim group, a gesture of kindness to a kid in Afghanistan, or a show of unity with Japanese atomic bomb survivors really mean anything? Who benefits from those connections? And what changes?

The answer, in most cases, is *me*. I change. And in doing so, I begin to achieve the change I want to see in the world. This is a concept I can wrap my brain around, even as I struggle to imagine how I can possibly make a difference in a world where force so thoroughly dominates our lives and our imaginations.

Indeed, gestures can go the other way, particularly gestures of violence. That kid in Afghanistan, or Iraq, or elsewhere along the so-called axis of evil: What transforming experiences will they recall from their encounters with us? What will they make of a glance, a word, or a tone of voice from the serviceman or -woman who might constitute their sole experience of Americans? What gentle touch will they recall from the bomb that destroyed their home or severed their arms? As I learned from meeting survivors of the bombings of Hiroshima and Nagasaki, anger can last decades. And as we've learned from the Oklahoma City bombing and the sniper attacks around Washington, DC, soldiers are also touched by violence across the years.

Thich Nhat Hanh, a Vietnamese Buddhist monk, notes, "When we train young people every day to kill, the damage is deep. They have known anger, they bear scars for many years. These kinds of wounds last for a long time and are transmitted to future generations. We cannot imagine the long-term effects of watering so many seeds of war."

We can also plant the seeds of peace, and nurture them, deliberately, because in the end I believe we have a choice to create the world we want to live in. So much of what we are told today, particularly about the "war on terrorism," is that we have no choices. This is a lie. Individuals have choices. Nations have choices. Freedom is about having choices, and when we stop having choices, we stop being free.

This is our choice: to make a gesture of kindness to a child in Afghanistan, or a mother in Iraq, or to a peace group in the United States, not to bear tangible results, not to change the world or to save them, so much as to save ourselves and create a moment. It is our gestures they will remember—for a minute, for an hour, for a lifetime. And those moments of peace, when strung together, will create a peaceful world.

I can't believe how completely wrongheaded you people are. First of all, you are quoting Martin Luther King completely out of context. His "wars are poor chisels . . ." comment was referring to a disagreement between Americans. That is, no matter how severe the disagreement we still had at our roots a shared set of values and a social contract. This gave us a starting place from which to have a discussion, and a peaceful way to pass his agenda of equal rights for all. Ironically enough, MLK would never have been able to make that speech in the first place if thousands of soldiers hadn't waged a war on his behalf.

*

Congratulations on being the "Jane Fondas for the Millenium" and I mean it in the worst possible conotation. Your position is deplorable and your actions are disgusting. You have no education regarding war and the need for defending our country. I am so glad that President Bush would not meet with you; you don't deserve the honor.

*

I think it's sad you lost family in the WTC, but your liberal, victim position in life is so tired I can't begin to write about how pathetic you look to those of us who live healthy, functional lives. You should have your citizenship revoked and be jetted out of this country. Luckily, the right to speak your uneducated opinion is protected . . . oh yeah, by the very types of individuals who did the bombing.

*

I think it would be great if no one hated anyone, no one was hungry or homeless, there was no greed or malice and each and every person respected the basic rights of others. I wish that were so. But, like my father used to say, wish in one hand and shit in the other, see which one fills up first. As long as I have to live in the real world I say God bless the U.S. Military!

*

Pushing people to a position where they have nothing to lose only gets more suicide bombs. Sitting comfortably in our homes sending our young to hunt and kill innocents is NOT the american way. For those who think that calling you unpatriotic or liberal is going to stop you, they don't have the faintest clue why AMERICA is #1!

*

You people are profoundly, BREATHTAKINGLY ignorant about history and basic human nature. First of all, violence has in fact solved an awful lot of problems. Small problems like the Third Reich, Imperial Japan and Soviet Communism were all solved either by violence or the threat of violence. Secondly, it only takes one side to make war but you need both sides to make peace. Since our enemies in this conflict have repeatedly stated that they want us all dead for the simple reason that we're not them, we don't really have any kind of common ground to start a dialogue on. You can love them as much as you want, they'll still kill you.

*

Refusing to fight and utterly capitulating to an enemy isn't "compassionate", it's cowardly. And condemning the poeple who protect you to stick up for people who want you dead is just plain stupid. Until you people come to your senses, I can only pray that you're in the path of the next bomb.

*Hope is a state of mind, not of the world . . . Hope, in
this deep and powerful sense, is not the same as joy that
things are going well, or willingness to invest in enterprises
that are obviously heading for . . . success, but rather an
ability to work for something because it is good.*
—Vaclav Havel, Czech dramatist, poet, and politician

Chapter Twelve

As summer gave way to fall, Peaceful Tomorrows had qualified
to become a project of the Tides Center, a San Francisco–based
organization providing fiscal sponsorship to progressive non-
profits. The handoff from FOR to Tides was an important emotional hurdle signifying forward momentum and validating the
seriousness with which the nonprofit and funding community
took Peaceful Tomorrows. Frances Anderson's video chronicling
the group's formation, *Steps to Peace,* had reached completion
and would be invaluable for raising public consciousness and
contributions.

These advances couldn't have come at a better time. With
the first commemoration of September 11 only weeks away,
members of Peaceful Tomorows, like others around the country
and the world, were struggling to identify an appropriate and
effective message. United for Peace, a new website created by
Global Exchange, would serve as a central hub for posting details
of events in hundreds of communities, demonstrating the depth
and diversity of peace sentiment in the country. Peaceful
Tomorrows would join in a united call for peaceful and healing
commemorations.

Recognizing their unique position, the family members
knew their activities would garner great attention, and that reality carried with it a tremendous sense of responsibility. But with
the anniversary stirring up deeply personal reactions, agreeing to

disagree remained a hallmark of the group's working style. And since the whole group couldn't commit to a single event, they did all of them. Kelly would organize a vigil in New York's Washington Square Park. Campbell and Barry Amundson would help organize and participate in several California events. Bodley and Rupp would be in Shanksville. Potorti, Olsen, and Ryan Amundson would participate in a "No More Victims" speaking tour with the AFSC. Matthew Lasar, Myrna Bethke, and other members would represent the group at commemorative events.

As it became clear that the family members would be scattered on September 11, the importance of being on the same page was clearer than ever. That made their first retreat as a group—at the Peace Abbey, in suburban Sherborn, Massachusetts—an invaluable opportunity to connect and to discuss a written statement expressing the group's feelings on the first anniversary of their loved ones' deaths. It was also an opportunity for the group to add three new members. Terry Rockefeller came to Peaceful Tomorrows by way of Phyllis Rodriguez's daughter, Julia, a professor who worked with Rockerfeller's husband, Bill Harris, at the University of New Hampshire. Terry lived in nearby Arlington, Massachusetts, and helped create and produce the long-running PBS science series *NOVA*, along with documentary films like *Eyes on the Prize* and a feature-length PBS documentary on democracy in Africa.

Terry's younger sister, Laura, happily following her bliss as an actress and singer in New York City, had a two-day job helping to run the conference on information technology that had drawn Bill Kelly, Jr. to Windows on the World on September 11. It was another sad bit of irony when they realized that Terry's sister might very well have met Colleen Kelly's brother that morning—and that neither one of them should have been there that day.

"The whole point of being an innocent victim is that there is no such thing as the wrong place at the wrong time—it's always the wrong place at the wrong time," Rockefeller said. "Because Laura didn't work at the World Trade Center, I really believed for a while after September 11 that if I could explain quite clearly to someone that she shouldn't have been there, that it somehow

Retreat at the Peace Abbey: signing cards with pewter hearts to family members who couldn't make it

would not have happened. There was something about making contact with Peaceful Tomorrows that made me get over the idea that it wasn't supposed to have happened to Laura. I could make that leap from 'This is not supposed to happen' to, 'We have to change the world in which this does happen.'"

Wright Salisbury, whose son-in-law, Ted Hennessy, Jr., died aboard American Airlines Flight 11 along with Kristina Olsen's sister, also joined the group. He had responded to the tragedy by creating a Center for Jewish-Christian-Muslim Understanding with the help of his church's Episcopal rector in Irvington, New York. Because his widowed daughter and her two small kids lived in Belmont, Massachusetts, Salisbury and his wife moved to nearby Lexington to be close to her, and shortly thereafter launched the Lexington Center for Jewish-Christian-Muslim Understanding—not far from the Peace Abbey.

Kathleen Tinley, from Council Bluffs, Iowa, was a pre-med student at Creighton University who in yet another ironic turn had lost her uncle Mike, a Marsh & McLennan officer based in Texas, at the World Trade Center—where he flown in for a meeting on the day of September 11. Tinley lived in the Spirit of Peace Community, an "intentional community" of like-minded souls striving to live lives of simplicity and reflection, and headed the local Pax Christi group at St. John's Parish. She had heard about Peaceful Tomorrows when Father John Dear, a Jesuit peace activist who had baptized Colleen Kelly's daughter, came to speak in her community. Tinley would later join the Peaceful Tomorrows delegation to Iraq.

One Year Later: September 11, 2002 Statement

For the members of Peaceful Tomorrows, September 11, 2001 was a day of unimaginable personal loss. Each of us lost a family member at the World Trade Center, at the Pentagon, or in the crash of Flight 93 near Shanksville, Pennsylvania. Losing loved ones to these extreme acts of violence has affected us deeply. It is something from which we will never recover, not in one year, not in a lifetime.

But in the days, weeks, and months following that terrible day of loss, we have also received incredible gifts. We gained each other—because we spoke out publicly about our opposition to war and violence as a response to our personal and national tragedies. We gained the love and compassion of new friends all over the United States and all over the world. And we gained the knowledge that there are thousands of Americans and millions around the globe who share our view that war is not the answer to the crimes of September 11.

The outpouring of support, compassion, and generosity our families have received has gone a long way toward filling the holes that were left in our hearts on that day, and we thank you. We would not be here today without your support.

We have also gained critics, and their criticism has given us another gift. It has made us consider what it means to be an American citizen. It has made us aware of our responsibilities. And it has made us realize that now, more than ever, the battle to defend our freedoms begins at home. We are all Americans. And if we cannot support each other, especially in our differences, then we have already lost this battle.

We have also come to recognize our kinship with other innocent victims of terrorism and war, a kinship that goes beyond our own borders. Among those who have reached out to us with sympathy are people who lost their own loved ones to violence throughout the world: people from Hiroshima and Nagasaki, Israel and the Palestinian territories, Afghanistan, Iran, Colombia, Ireland, and others who have experienced horrific losses. They have welcomed us into their global family, and we treasure their support.

For us, September 11 was a day when the walls came down. It was a day when we realized that there were no barricades high enough, no bombs big enough, and no intelligence sophisticated enough to prolong the illusion of American invulnerability.

Since that day, it has become clear to us that America must fully participate in the global community: by honoring international treaties, endorsing and participating in the international criminal court, following the United Nations charter, and agreeing in word and action to the precepts of international law. This is vital, if peace and justice are to prevail everywhere on earth, including in our own country.

The deepened awareness that America is an integral part of a shared globe is central to Peaceful Tomorrows' mission. America no longer has the option of acting unilaterally. We live in the 21st century, in an age when the barriers to trade and to the exchange of goods, services, ideas, and people are disappearing. This reality brings with it the urgent need for new ways of dealing with the rest of the world. We must move beyond seeking revenge and instead seek accountability for actions that foster violence. We must conquer injustice by creating a just world. We—and our children and grandchildren—will live in a connected world. We can no longer pretend to live outside of it.

But a year after September 11, 2001, we wonder how our loved ones lost on that day would feel about what has been done in their names. What would they think of our rush to military action? What would they think of the diminishing of our personal freedoms and civil liberties? And what would they think about the results of our choices?

More than forty American service people have died in the military campaign in Afghanistan. Yet the few successful apprehensions of known Al-Qaeda members have been made by other nations, through police actions, intelligence, and diplomatic channels.

In Afghanistan, thousands of innocent civilians have been affected by the bombing, and the lives of millions remain in danger from the ongoing hunger and poverty resulting from two decades of war, exacerbated by our recent military operations. Members of Peaceful Tomorrows have visited innocent Afghan families who lost loved ones in the U.S. bombing. We have campaigned for assistance to these families, believing that such assistance represents the highest ideals of America and serves to bolster our support in the region.

Still, the interim government of Kabul remains unstable, and the progress made for women in Afghanistan remains uncertain. In the June 16, 2002 issue of the *New York Times,* officials of the FBI and CIA acknowledged that the bombing of Afghanistan did not make America safer, and may have in fact complicated antiterrorism efforts by dispersing Al-Qaeda elements to other countries.

The contemplated invasion of Iraq—a nation that has no proven links to the events of September 11—in the name of the "war on terrorism" means that more American service people and more civilians would die, with unforeseen effects on our security, our economy, our ability to address the root causes of terrorism, and our relationship with other nations.

At home, the consequences of our singular reliance on a military response to the tragedies of 9/11 have been far-reaching. Our nation has yet to begin a meaningful, independent investigation of how and why the September 11 attacks occurred, information that is crucial for protecting us from similar attacks in the future. Our domestic problems—unemployment, inadequate health care, poor schools, and hunger—continue to grow, as does our military budget.

The war on terrorism does not put reality on hold. It is time to acknowledge that pursuing a military response in the absence of pursuing other options is an extravagantly expensive, wasteful, and limited means of action. The real work begins when the bombs stop dropping.

Terrorism is portrayed as our greatest, newest problem. But it is also a symptom rooted in other, more familiar problems: Extremism. Militarism. Poverty. Racism. Ignorance. Inequality. Hatred. Hopelessness. Rage. We haven't done enough to address them. And until we do, they will continue to announce their presence through violence and terrorism, in an increasingly desperate attempt to bring about change.

We believe it is time to stop dropping bombs and to start paying attention. To start asking difficult questions. To start listening to a multitude of voices. And to start exploring—and using—effective alternatives to war.

Today, members of Peaceful Tomorrows fear that our country is heading in the wrong direction. But we hope that through vigorous dialogue and a willingness to question and critique our actions we can begin to right our course. And we must—in the names of our lost loved ones, in the names of our families, and in the names of yours. No other family, anywhere on earth, should have to experience the pain and loss we experienced on September 11.

Our critics tell us that America is great because it is powerful. We think America is powerful because it is great. We believe America is great because of its freedoms, its values, its Constitution, and its diversity of opinion. We believe America possesses not only military strength, but a host of other strengths: legal strength, moral strength, spiritual and intellectual strength. We believe that all of these strengths must be utilized. And we believe that in a democracy, we all serve, not just our men and women in uniform.

On September 11, 2002, we invite our fellow citizens to affirm their love of country, to honor those who were lost on this day one year ago, and to mourn the loss of life to violence throughout the world. We ask that the commemoration of September 11 serve as a call for peace and healing, not for more war and violence. And we ask you to bring your own unique skills and talents to bear in a critical national dialogue.

Only by including all of our voices will we find a path to justice. And only through justice will we find peace: peace for ourselves and for all Americans, grieving the loss of innocent family members, friends, and co-workers on September 11. Peace for Afghan families, grieving the loss of loved ones in the U.S.-led bombing campaign and in the preceding twenty-three years of war.

And, peace for our counterparts around the world—the other families who have experienced violence. We recognize them as our brothers and sisters, our mothers and fathers, our children and our grandchildren. If the September 11 deaths of nearly three thousand Americans representing eighty nationalities teach us anything, it is that we are connected. Our grief is their grief. Our world is their world. And our destiny is their destiny.

* * *

On Friday, September 6, 2002, Potorti boarded a plane for Philadelphia for what would be the first stop in the joint Peaceful Tomorrows/AFSC "No More Victims Tour." Billed as "placing the human dimension and experience of the 9/11 attacks and of war at the center of the national debate over the 'war against terrorism,'" the ten-day tour would initiate with Potorti, move on to Olsen, and then to Ryan Amundson and Kathleen Tinley, who would speak for the first time as a member of Peaceful Tomorrows.

Their testimonies would be amplified by those of Rangina Hamidi, an Afghan-American who had twice returned to Afghanistan to provide assistance since the U.S. war began last fall; Sinan Antoon, an Iraqi living in Boston; Ms. Amirah Ali Lidasan, secretary general of the Moro Christian People's Alliance in Mindinao, Philippines; and Miyoko Matsubara, a leading Japanese *hibakusha* from Hiroshima. Nevertheless, the first question of the tour, at a Philadelphia press conference, was,

No More Victims Tour: David Potorti, Miyoko Matsubara,
Joseph Gerson (AFSC), Amirah Ali Lidasan, and Sinan Antoon

"Do you think the Bush Administration is taking advantage of September 11 to rally support for war in Iraq?"

The first speaking event, which took place at the Foundation for Islamic Education in Villanova, Pennsylvania, began with a potluck dinner for both audience and speakers, making clear the power of food to unite cultures. A Boston event took place at historic Faneuil Hall, in sight of a balcony from which the Declaration of Independence was read in 1776. In Northampton, Massachusetts, a crowd of 2,500 assembled to hear Kristina Olsen sing "The Art of Being Kind," before joining the speaking panel. In every case, powerful connections were made, and tears flowed.

* * *

In New York City, the crazy quilt of race, nationality, politics, and style that provides the town with its peculiar energy and tension was everywhere evident in the peace movement. But somehow the emotions of the city, at that time, magnified differences, personalities, and outcomes. Months of hashing over plans for one unified event around 9/11 had, like the internal discussions within Peaceful Tomorrows itself, ended with plans for multiple events that would occur under the banner of "Stand Up New York."

Among the ideas under discussion: a "reverse exodus," recalling the flight of terrified New Yorkers by foot that day, which would feature marches over the Brooklyn and Williamsburg Bridges into, rather than out of, the city, and ending in Union Square Park; individual rallies in neighborhoods throughout the city, which would ultimately join together; symbolic events like floating lanterns on the East River to commemorate the dead; and die-ins to symbolize the dead not only from the events of 9/11 but from "endless wars."

Kristina Olsen opens the No More Victims Tour
at historic Faneuil Hall in Boston

Ultimately, Peaceful Tomorrows and a host of others, referring to themselves as "the vigil committee," split from the rest of
the group over the tone of the event: They wanted a vigil, focusing on grief and compassion and honoring the dead of 9/11. "We
don't hold one event as 'better' than the other," the committee
wrote in an e-mail. "These are simply two very valid responses to
what is going on in this world, and our hope is that between both
events, a vast majority of the public can feel compelled to attend
at least one."

War Resisters League, Peaceful Tomorrows, Pax Christi,
FOR, the AFSC, Peace Action, Jews for Racial and Economic
Justice, The Women's International League for Peace and
Freedom, and Global Exchange, along with Islamic and South
Asian community groups, organized a "peace commemoration"
that would counteract the "patriotic delerium" afflicting the rest
of the city and the nation. The plan called for music and
speeches in Washington Square Park on the evening of
September 10, an all-night vigil, a resumption of speeches and
music on the morning of the 11th, a moment of silence at 8:46
A.M., the time when the first plane hit the World Trade Center,
and silent marches throughout the city to keep the notion of
peace in the public eye throughout the day.

"The tone will be reverent and respectful," read the invitation sent to potential speakers. "Resolute in our desire for true
peace, this will not be an occasion for political invective, but
rather a time to find the spiritual sobriety—the hope—that genuine mourning can bring."

In addition to a delegation of Peaceful Tomorrows members,
speakers would include Manning Marable, director of the
Institute for Research in African-American Studies at Columbia
University; Michael Ratner, of the Center for Constitutional
Rights and an attorney for Guantánamo detainees; the Muslim
American Society's Debbie Almontaser; longtime activist priest

Father Daniel Berrigan; Israeli Terza Even, from New Profile; Cambodian refugee and author Luong Ung; anti-globalization activist Reverend Billy; musicians, including Pat Humphries, Sandy Opatow, the LaGuardia High School Chorale (courtesy of Muhammed Ali and the Ali Center); and familiar friends, such as Amy Goodman, Kathy Kelly, and Masuda Sultan. The evening would be crowned with a speech by Martin Luther King, III.

* * *

Meg Bartlett, an EMT worker with a private ambulance company who had been sent to the World Trade Center site in a futile attempt to rescue survivors, would also speak publicly for the first time at the vigil that night. Her experience of the tragedy compelled her to launch a group called Ground Zero for Peace/ First Responders Against War.

"My first thought wasn't about war, it was about violence, and that there definitely has to be an end to this," Bartlett said of her arrival at the site. "I was looking at firemen and cops coming out of the pit, and thinking that no one on the planet should have to see this stuff. And then I realized that people all around the world see this stuff on a much more regular basis than we do, and they shouldn't have to see it, either." Intent on doing her job, she didn't even watch the news until that night, and only then recognized the larger implications.

"I remember thinking, 'Oh my god, our country is going to make people pay for this forever,'" she said. "And there seemed to be a difference—it didn't seem like justice we were after, it felt like pure revenge. And it scared me, because all that does is create more situations where people have to look at what I just saw. I thought of it in terms of showing up to a car accident—I don't stop to say, 'Are you from my country, do you share my faith, where were your parents born?' I do what I can to save the peo-

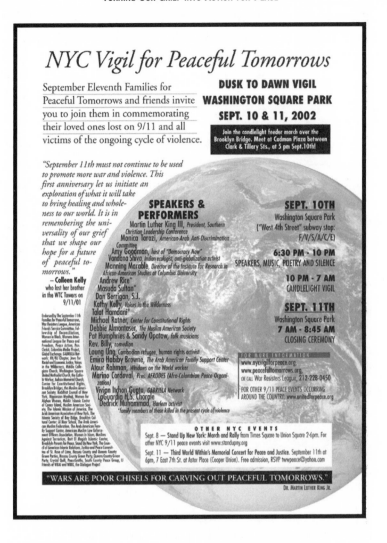

ple's lives. As an EMT, it made no sense that we should support the creation of more death, when our job was to save lives."

Wanting to organize first-responders who felt the same way, she randomly struck up conversations at firehouses, or at parked ambulances, or with co-workers, to explore what people were thinking.

"I realized that very few people felt the way that I felt," she reported. "They would say, 'I think we have to go into

Afghanistan, we have to go after bin Laden,' but they would also say, 'I happen to know a guy who might think along your lines, here's his number.'" It took months to get a loosely organized group of eight people who would publicly say they belonged to the Ground Zero group.

"Our community—uniformed police, firefighters, EMS workers—was absolutely shattered," Bartlett said. "When you lose a family member, the world understands how to rally behind you, but when you lose co-workers, it's not as clear. When you have a job that takes so many hours, or you live in a firehouse, or you spend two shifts a day on an ambulance, those *are* your family members. Co-workers are extremely important—they save your life on a regular basis. Because of that deep-seated loss, and grief, and anger, I sometimes think we were the most terrified group of anyone—because, while the rest of the country was terrorized, we had the visuals to go along with it. And I think that posed particular challenges to organizing—it was so difficult, with the heightened sense of terrorism and sense of responsibility, to make sure something like that didn't happen again. That's an incredible amount of pressure, and it almost doesn't give you the head space to think about organizing with others."

Fear, she said, remained a motivating factor.

"One of my friends said that when it really comes down to it, the inside of a body looks the same no matter what continent it's found on," she recalled. "But because he feels so scared, he has to get behind the war. And these are good, brave men. All the men I work with do amazing things every day, and really care about people deeply. It's not like they're personally afraid—it's like a culture of fear that we live in now."

* * *

On September 8, a Walk for Healing and Peace took place, this time around Lake Merritt in Oakland, California and with the help of Campbell and Barry Amundson. The event was hosted by the Islamic Cultural Center of Northern California and American Muslims Intent on Learning and Activism (AMILA), and drew about three hundred sign-carrying participants. Later, Campell spoke at the Cultural Center, along with poets, teenage girls reading passages from the Quran, and several Imams, one of whom had joined Olsen and Bethke on their June trip to Afghanistan. Like the Villanova event, food played a major role in cementing friendship: The cultural center had hosted "A Night in Tehran" the previous evening, and the participants— largely Iranian—were the beneficiaries of leftovers. Two days later, Rita Lasar's son, Matthew, would speak at a lantern-floating ceremony on the Lake.

Campbell and Amundson flew to Los Angeles on September 9 and 10 for "A Gathering for Civil Liberties and Peaceful Tomorrows," co-sponsored by a number of groups and individuals including Southern California Americans for Democratic Action, Interfaith Communities, United for Peace and Justice, the Nation Institute, Liberty Hill, Tom Hayden, and Progressive Religious Partnership. "After Craig was killed, there were so many memorials that turned into war rallies," Campbell said. "This September 11, we wanted there to be alternatives that looked at where we go as Americans, and where we go as human beings."

At the downtown First Baptist Church, an audience of 1,200 viewed *Steps to Peace* and heard from speakers including Campbell, Medea Benjamin, Robert Scheer, and leading Islamic, Jewish, and Christian clerics, including Reverend Jim Lawson, a colleague of Martin Luther King, Jr., who trained an entire generation of activists in methods of nonviolent direct action. "All patriotic Americans ought to be drawn to places like this," he said. "Justice is to peace as oxygen is to breathing."

Alfre Woodard read passages from a variety of religious scriptures, gospel singer Brenda Marie Eager moved the crowd with "I Ain't Gonna Study War No More," and Medea Benjamin brought the house to its feet with a call for "regime change here at home."

Campbell and Amundson accepted an award from the LA City Council, and spoke to seven television stations at a press conference that followed, demonstrating intense interest in peaceful responses to September 11, even thousands of miles from Ground Zero.

"We made a lot of connections," Campbell said, "including a woman who worked with families of the disappeared from Central America, and a young Muslim woman who had also lost her brother to violence. She said, 'Thank you for reminding me that people are good at heart.' She had forgotten that during the past year, and needed to hear it."

* * *

To suggest that New York was a city on edge in the days leading up to September 11, 2002 would be a profound understatement. For many, the events of a year earlier seemed like yesterday, a feeling reinforced by the weather itself—the week was shaping up to be sunny and cloudless, just as it had been on that tragic day. Personal grief would be overshadowed by public ceremony— thousands of representatives of the international press, members of Congress, and, of course, the President, would appear, along with ferociously heightened security that included helicopter gunships patrolling the city. While security precautions were an unavoidable necessity, New Yorkers of all stripes were, on some level, experiencing what could only be described as post-traumatic stress. And that only begins to describe the state of mind of the thousands who would come to New York to visit Ground Zero and relive the murders of their wives, husbands, fathers, mothers, brothers, sisters, and children.

But on the evening of September 10, the Vigil for Peaceful Tomorrows attempted to create a space for healing and reflection. As the family members gathered, many of them meeting for the first time, Terry Rockefeller got a tap on the shoulder from Andrew Rice, and the two of them realized they had met several times before: Rice and his sister, Amy, had made a film

*Vigil for Peaceful Tomorrows: Andrew Rice, Myrna Bethke,
Colleen Kelly, and Dan Jones, September 10, 2002*

with a mutual friend. "I turned around and came face-to-face
with this person I knew," Rockefeller said. "And I didn't know
that his brother had been killed. It was shocking." It was also a
reminder of the connections shared before—and after—
September 11.

As people on foot eventually coalesced into a crowd estimated
at five thousand, the evening commenced with music and a series
of powerful religious invocations. Rice represented the group as
he spoke to a theme of reconciliation and valuing all victims of
violence and war in the same way. Myrna Bethke, Dan Jones,
Colleen Kelly, David Potorti, and Terry Rockefeller held hands in
a semicircle behind him, bearing poignant witness to their losses
and their public response.

Bartlett found her public appearance as the founder of
Ground Zero for Peace/First Responders Against War that night
to be personally redeeming.

"A lot of times people think that because we want a peaceful
resolution, we don't care as much for the people that died, and
that couldn't be father from the truth," she said. "So it was really
nice to tell the families that those of us who were on the ground,
the workers, cops, at the bottom of the ladder, we really did our

best, we performed exceedingly well, and we did everything we could. In our job, we usually go into a situation where other people are scared, or you go to somebody that's sick, and their families are counting on you to take control of the situation and do everything you can. To be sent into a situation on September 11 where you were clearly, clearly not in control, was personally terrifying. Organizing my group helped me to get a sense of control back, a feeling that I could be effective."

* * *

Throughout the evening, peace activities took place across the park: Participants could make Japanese lanterns, or paper cranes; the World Peace Pole provided spaces for prayers to be added; markers and paint were on hand for those who felt moved to draw or to write messages; music—from a classical string quartet to Tibetan drumming to chanting—drifted through the park.

As the evening wore on, King remained a wild card. That created a problem: Weighing the public importance of the occasion against the needs of the private residences surrounding the park, the neighborhood police had granted a sound permit until 10 P.M. only, though allowing park activities—the folding of peace cranes, creation of banners, lessons in meditation—to continue into the night. But due to a delayed plane, it became clear that King would not arrive until after the sound curfew. A deal was struck with the police department, allowing the sound to go back on long enough for King to speak.

Talat Hamdani, a Pakistani-American English teacher from Queens, New York, and one of the newest members of Peaceful Tomorrows, bore moving witness to the loss of her son, Mohammed Salman Hamdani, a 23-year-old New York Police Department cadet, who disappeared after the tragedy and—having a Pakistani name—was wrongfully accused of participating in the terrorist attacks. His body was recovered and identified in March 2002, affirming what his mother had asserted for months: Salman died trying to help others at the World Trade Center. Closing the formal ceremony, his grieving mother began a candle-lighting ceremony—the flame going from one candle to another—that spread throughout the park.

* * *

Talat Hamdani's speech, delivered by her son, Zeshan, at the first Osborn Elliott Community Leadership Awards ceremony, honoring Mohammed Salman Hamdani.

Dear Friends and Fellow Citizens:

While my son is being honored, I find myself in total submission to my God. My life took a drastic turn on September 11, and I am forced to make sense out of this heinous crime against civilization. I am unable to answer why it happened or who is ultimately responsible.

But, I know for sure that Islam is not responsible for this crime. The ignorant people who distort Islam or who maintain that Islam preaches to kill, should read the Quran themselves and discover how merciful and forgiving this religion is.

I would like to clarify the meaning of the word JIHAD, a grossly misunderstood term. It means "struggle," or "crusade." Terrorism is no crusade . . . Don't accept the perversion of this concept. As President Bush said, the terrorists have hijacked a religion.

Salman's death has given me a mission—to wage jihad against terrorism and ignorance, a crusade for understanding. We can rise above terrorism, ignorance, and discrimination through education, tolerance, forgiveness, and, like Salman, noble acts.

Salman was a casualty of 9/11 not because he was an EMT, an NYPD cadet, or a Muslim-American of Pakistani descent. He was a casualty of 9/11 because he was an American who went down to the Twin Towers to save his fellow Americans regardless of their skin color, ethnicity, or religious beliefs.

I believe such tragic moments define and shape a nation. The phoenix rises from its ashes stronger and purified. From the

The Interfaith Center of New York
and
The Temple of Understanding

request your presence at

The Annual Interfaith Service of Commitment to the Work of the United Nations

A Celebration of Remembrance and Hope
Dedicated to Victims of Violence Everywhere

To mark the opening of the
57th Session of the United Nations General Assembly

Special Guests include
President of the General Assembly Mr. Jan Kavan
Secretary-General Kofi Annan and Mrs. Nane Annan
September Eleventh Families for Peaceful Tomorrows

Wednesday, September 11, 2002
at 8:30 a.m.

St. Bartholomew's Church
Park Avenue at 51st Street

Please be seated by 8:15 a.m.
The service will conclude before 10 a.m.

For security reasons, no packages will be allowed in the church.
This card must be presented at the door for admittance.

The Interfaith Center of New York · 40 East 30th Street · New York, NY 10016 · 212-685-4242

ashes of 9/11 America will, Inshallah, rise a stronger, more civilized, and more tolerant nation. An America that accepts and welcomes all of its citizens.

Thank you, and may God bless us—and America. Ameen.

* * *

When Martin Luther King, III arrived at 10:45 P.M., he succeeded in galvanizing the crowd with a reminder that was all too easy to forget: He, too, was a victim of terrorism, having lost his father to the gun of a domestic terrorist.

As evening gave way to the first minutes of September 11, there remained a pervasive sense of fellowship as different faith traditions quietly performed their own symbolic rituals of mourning in various corners of the park. A reading of the names of 9/11 victims—as well as people who had also died in Afghanistan and Iraq—continued through the morning hours. Project Liberty (a New York City mental-health service) remained on hand to counsel anyone who needed help.

Kelly and seventy other vigilers stayed throughout the night. At dawn, they were joined by a peace group that had walked from Schenectady, New York—a distance of 170 miles—to honor 9/11 victims. At 8:46 A.M.—the time that the first plane hit the World Trade Center a year earlier—Buddhist clerics led a crowd of several hundred in a silent prayer.

"There was so much joy in knowing there were so many people in the city who wanted to commemorate September 11 in a nonviolent way," Kelly said. "And on a personal level, knowing that so many people cared about our loved ones, cared enough about people they didn't know, that they would come to an event like this."

* * *

Later that morning, Rice, Potorti, and Bethke made their way to the World Trade Center site. Peaceful Tomorrows, UN Secretary General Kofi Annan, and UN President Jan Kavan were feted at the annual prayer service, hosted by the Interfaith Center of New York and the Temple of Understanding at St. Bartholomew's Church, that signaled the start of the new UN session. Kelly would speak on behalf of the group, and her family, along with Bethke and Rockefeller, were present to show their support for the international institution that honored their group.

That afternoon, Rice was scheduled to speak at a UN conference on the role of religion and healing in response to violence. It would be cancelled due to threats of violence against the panelists.

* * *

Later that day in Shanksville, Pennsylvania, Eva Rupp, Derrill Bodley, his wife, and the families of all of those lost on Flight 93 prepared for the arrival of President Bush.

"I felt a sort of connection with all the families that were there," Rupp said. "I read the book about all the passengers. I tried to read everything about the flight, because I felt like I had to know who was there, and what had happened. To meet the families was really powerful, to all be together was powerful. But it was a difficult day."

"It was all I could do to keep from walking out as 'The Battle Hymn of the Republic'—all four verses—was sung at the public part of the service," Bodley said. "This brutal song's fourth verse called on us to invoke Jesus Christ's name and proselytizing as we waged war."

> *In the beauty of the lilies*
> *Christ was born across the sea,*
> *With a glory in His bosom*
> *That transfigures you and me;*
> *As He died to make men holy,*
> *Let us die to make men free;*
> *While God is marching on.*

"On a day of remembrance, the feelings inside each of us needed to be reconciled, not inflamed," Bodley said. "I still don't know why this song was selected. I wonder what the Buddhists, Jews, and people of other non-Christian faiths, including some

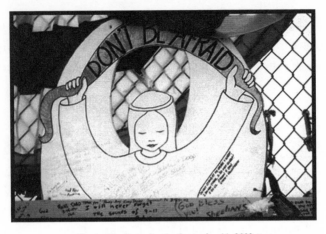

Shanksville, Pennsylvania, September 11, 2002

of the family members for whom the memorial was held, were thinking when they heard it."

The families watched as a helicopter landed in a field, kicking up dust. President Bush and the First Lady drove up a secured road and emerged for handshakes and photos with the families. As Bodley took the President's hand, he said, "Mr. President, I urge you to listen to the world leaders who are strongly advising against going down the path of war."

EXTENDING OUR MOMENT TOWARD REPAIR
by Andrew Rice

Either we are doing good and this good does not persuade, or we are perceived to have done ill and this ill must be repented. At this crossover moment in history, we must be as self-critical as we are critical of the terrorists. We must ask how all of this came to be. We must ask why so many people are listening to a man we know as extreme, maybe even insane with power.

—Sister Joan Chittister, *Sojourners Magazine,* Fall 2001

When President George W. Bush spoke at the National Cathedral in Washington, DC just days after the terrorist violence that killed, among thousands of others, my older brother, David, there was a moment when he appeared to be rising to the occasion to face the tragedy head-on and deal with its implications humbly. He showed tremendous compassion and rightly honored the everyday people who had been unjustly murdered, and praised those who risked their lives to save others. His tone was a somber one. However, soon into his speech his talk turned defiant, and he shirked the responsibility of every courageous leader to deal fully with the truths of such a conflict, both the difficult ones and the comforting ones. It was his responsibility, to us, his citizens, if no one else.

His speech was at times religious, yet it was often coupled with a striking irreligious tone that suggested, as Americans, we have divine entitlement to retaliate, rather than a just pursuit of the terrorists free from revenge. The President said:

> America is a nation full of good fortune, with so much to be grateful for. But we are not spared from suffering. In every generation, the world has produced enemies of human freedom. They have attacked America, because we are freedom's home and defender. And the commitment of our fathers is now the calling of our time.
>
> War has been waged against us by stealth and deceit and murder. This nation is peaceful, but fierce when stirred to anger. This conflict was begun on the timing and terms of others. It will end in a way, and at an hour, of our choosing.

President Bush's tone on that day and after has indelibly shaped a mainstream understanding of the September 11 attacks that has ultimately had devastating consequences on our hopes of truly preventing future terrorism, and has in turn led to the compulsion to inflict tragedies upon scores of others as we wildly strike back out of anger and anxiety. He has irresponsibly given a fearful and shaken nation the permission to stay blind to the sorrowful world that helped give rise to the attacks.

That fragile time period held out for us a golden moment where a non-retributive American response to 9/11 would have stood as a shining example on the world stage, and could have paved the way for measured and humane responses to other conflicts as well. Instead of now modeling arrogant "pre-emptive self-defense" for the likes of Pakistan and India, we could be demonstrating restraint and a commitment to the principles of international law. Our credibility would have been immeasurable. The display of moral courage would have been historic: the sole superpower, capable of all means of retaliation, instead choosing to seek justice through international institutions designed to peacefully and justly redress such tragedies as September 11.

This moment was an unprecedented one for an American leader, and the chance to rise up to the highest part of our humanity was missed. This was our crossover moment in time, and many everyday citizens have taken up the call for a conciliatory and non-militaristic response to what was in reality a crime against humanity, not an act of war. We could have dealt bravely with the very real dangers of the world by taking on the challenge of breaking the cycle of self-interest and retaliation already set in motion years earlier. Our moment has not passed, and we can yet reclaim the principle of human rights and the power of nonviolent change that can, in fact, create a world where the burning and hopeless desperation to commit terrorist acts is less alluring. This is where the real solution to terrorism lies.

Could President Bush have given any other speech that sad day in September? Many historians argue that any leader of what we call a "great nation" (which in this context really means a *powerful* nation) must show a defiant face to tyranny and injustice when attacked as we were. Many argue that reaching across the dark divide between us and the terrorists, to ask difficult questions as we rightly condemned the senseless violence, would have been unthinkable and would have excused the barbarity of the attacks. Yet, many in this nation and world were yearning for such clarity and strength as we tried to grieve the dead. We needed to make sense of the devastation and hatred. The dehumanization of the terrorists into "evildoers" who hate "freedom's home" has not only led to dangerous and arrogant policies, it has also left the nation's anxiety mostly unchanged and buried just underneath a facade of patriotic flag-waving, righteousness, and fear-based muscularity.

We needed truthful explanations about why troubled and angry young men, with mothers and families, were willing to kill themselves and thousands of innocent people. This analysis of motives—which is the normal protocol for investigating crimes—would help us find ways to extinguish the fire that fuels their hatred, rather than endlessly trying to extinguish "terrorists" and the next generation who may possibly become them. Can't we avoid this hopeless and seemingly endless cycle of violent campaigns that give us and them a false sense of meaning and empowerment?

Such an act of humility and resolve would have opened the door for a new era in world politics, and would have perhaps saved many people from the traumas and horrors of war that followed, as well as those that lurk on the horizon. Undoubtedly this process would not be easy or simple. However, it would have steered us away from the hysterical machinations that have stripped many people of their basic human rights here and abroad. It could have spurred a serious rethinking of American foreign policy that can much more effectively take the air out of terrorist grievances than any smart bomb or cowboy threat could hope to do. It would have taught our children and the world that an unjustly suffering nation can trudge forward toward justice while avoiding the twin temptations of prideful retribution and denial.

Such hopes and aspirations are dismissed as idealistic by those who have lost faith both in human dignity and the power of courageous love. While we celebrate the birthdays of figures like King and Gandhi, many now claim their messages of forgiveness are not applicable. We lauded Tutu and Mandela for their tremendous efforts at reconciliation, but now some of the more powerful among us like to dismiss their historical lessons as irrelevant.

In the most spiritual sense of the word, redemption is the process toward repairing or restoring something that is broken. We are without a doubt still in disrepair from that day and the invisible days before it, and more havoc has been wrought in the months since—both to us and by us. September 11 was not the beginning of a conflict, as many of our most influential opinion-makers are fond of arguing. Rather, that day was a jarring and horrific confrontation with a damaged world that we were already in conflict with. It was not a day that changed the world—although it undoubtedly changed *our* world here in America. It was a day that ushered us into the human family more fully. And this is a sad and difficult reality to face.

Living in a nation that never anticipated having to deal with something like September 11 is on the surface ideal and reassuring. It projects a society that is optimistic and free, and believes in the ideals on which it was founded. And in turn, such a society feels such values would logically find themselves being played out in our relations with everyone, everywhere. Of course, many of us know this to be untrue, though by no means a defect intrinsic only to America. Most great powers realize that placing the interests of others on par with their own causes problems with their need to sustain the very power with which they are so obsessed.

Therefore, America has needed a highly misinformed public to believe in the fairy-tale depiction of its history. It is no surprise that many Americans were "shocked" that September 11 actually happened, which is unique from the shock at the enormous scale of the attacks. This idea that the attacks "came out of nowhere" exposes how detached many of us were, and still are, from the reality of a world that can be ugly and unfair, and replete with suffering. It reveals how many in America have been visibly and emotionally cut off from those with whom we all are in a very close relationship. America is the royal family of an unbalanced, globalized world. Like any royalty, many of us have had remarkable ignorance about the "subjects" of the world community who both love and hate us. And for so long we were "protected" from the consequences of this relationship. September 11 showed that to be a false sense of security.

Belief in this fallacy, however, remains. We watch war on television like it's the Olympics, and then get in our cars and drive to the store. The world is for our viewing, as if we are not participants in it. It's a strange position to be in: to have such economic, military, and cultural power over others, yet be so unaware of the consequences it can have in their daily lives. And then ultimately not see how it in turn plays out in *our* lives down the road. We may have power, but we are in other more existential ways scared to look directly at what it really stands for, therefore it dramatically coincides with a certain uneasiness and denial that is the converse of power. It is a contradiction of being powerful: to on the one hand relish the rewards of dominance, yet on the other hand not have the psychological fortitude to look at the injustice it often breeds.

The thrust of opposition to our country comes mostly from a rebellion toward our power, more than an enmity for our culture. The latter is surely a factor in the ideology that fuels groups like Al-Qaeda, but it alone is not what makes angry men willing to kill themselves and other people. September 11 was much more about power and geo-political politics than it was about dislike for our liberal democracy.

However, being hated for "who we are" is indeed more comforting than looking at the messiness of how individuals with some understandable angers can in turn act on them in such deplorable ways. And as the predominant explanation for our woes, it pragmatically allows the few and powerful to avoid changing the "what we do" that in reality spurs anti-Americanism, while keeping an American majority cozy in its apathy.

Grossly misunderstanding the reasons for anti-American anger, whether it be that of the French or of Al-Qaeda, becomes easy when we see our country's presence in the world as some sort of wholly innocuous and benevolent power that has successfully rejected the compulsion for global inequity that is inherent to all empires. Seeing American power as a type of altruistic force, as a repository of goodness for others, is a long-standing archetype of our collective psyche, which is part and parcel of any empire.

Contrary to the popular and simplistic rhetoric that depicts a purely altruistic and principled America faced with an irredeemably evil enemy, we are instead mired in something far more complex. Until the leaders and opinion-makers of this nation accept the crucial distinction between terrorist grievances and their methods of avenging them, we will remain embroiled in the current apocalyptic crusade to rid the world of evil. Terrorist methods are abhorrent. Terrorist grievances, on the other hand, are almost always an outgrowth of messy political and cultural conflicts the likes of which are rarely resolved effectively with armies.

To my mind, nothing could repair our broken relationship more than advancing our societies to where the hateful extremists and intransigent elitists are isolated on the fringes of our great and sensible societies. Their violent methods will become antiquated and easily ridiculed—though with compassion. At present, these two sides—the fanatics and the superpower elites—have constituencies who hopelessly accept the violent means which they employ, and which disproportionately kill the citizens of the world rather than each other. We are caught in the middle.

The overwhelming majority of the victims killed on September 11, and the two wars that followed, are not the people making the extreme decisions. Redeeming these tragedies is the responsibility of us caught in the crossfire. We are the ones who will pull conflict resolution and diplomacy from the margins back onto the center-stage of international affairs. We are the ones who will, in the midst of our sadness and regret, approach each other asking and granting forgiveness. We are the ones who will demonstrate that we can break through denial and wrestle with the truth of our conflicts. This is our crossover moment in time, and we will not make the journey to the other side by creating more victims. We will make it there by not abandoning our principles when they become inconvenient.

Our children deserve a world without end. Not a war without end. Our children deserve a world free of the terror of hunger, free of the terror of poor healthcare, free of the terror of homelessness, free of the terror of ignorance, free of the terror of hopelessness, free of the terror of policies which are committed to a worldview which is not appropriate for the survival of a free people, not appropriate for the survival of democratic values, not appropriate for the survival of our nation, and not appropriate for the survival of the world.

—Congressman Dennis Kucinich, "A Prayer for America"

Chapter Thirteen

For members of Peaceful Tomorrows, the days following September 11, 2002 produced a not-unexpected tidal wave of emotions, a sense of letdown and genuine exhaustion. The dead had been given their due—now it was time for the living to bring themselves back to life.

"It was the first time I felt like I had gotten past something," Rockefeller said of the commemoration. "There are so many ways in which I miss Laura more now, because that first year I was doing everything: I filed all the papers, dealt with all the bureaucracies, had to sue the workers'-compensation board because the people who hired Laura to work at the conference said she wasn't an employee (she won, after three hearings). But now, life is kind of back to normal—I'm not going from crisis to crisis anymore, and now I just miss her. It's totally irrational, but sometimes I think if I just take care of every little last bit of bureaucracy, she'll come back."

"Peaceful Tomorrows has helped me grieve," said Andrew Rice. "I still have deep anger that my brother was killed so brutally—both because I selfishly do not have him here anymore, and at the basic injustice of his death. If I did not have an outlet for all of this energy, I don't know what I would do. Being able to work toward having good things come out of September 11, and opposing the bad things, of which there are many, I feel like David's death was not in vain."

With military action in Iraq appearing more and more inevitable, the group wrote another letter to the President. "We are disappointed that you have used the anniversary of our loved ones' deaths not as a time to mourn and reflect but as a time to call for war on a country unrelated to the events of September 11," they said. "We are concerned that a war in Iraq will divert the necessary resources from the task of apprehending and bringing to justice those responsible for the September 11 attacks. We fear this war could destabilize the Middle East region and cost the lives of countless innocent civilians in other nations. We are deeply troubled that more killing will only fuel the fires of terrorism and enable terrorist organizations to recruit more easily those who would harm us."

Meanwhile, Colleen Kelly explored the possibility of organizing a Peaceful Tomorrows delegation to meet with Iraqi civilians. Like the delegation to Afghanistan, it was intended to humanize the plight of the Iraqi people, who had known war, suffered under the terror of a dictatorial regime, and, according to UNICEF, had lost half a million of their children to the effects of economic sanctions. In so doing, the delegation hoped to slow the rush to war and increase the likelihood that weapons inspectors would be given the time needed to address the question of whether military action was necessary. In fact, there were already delegations from thirty-two countries in Iraq—peace groups, aid groups, religious groups—many with the same mission.

Because the group wanted to invite sympathetic members of Congress to join them, Kelly faxed a letter to Ohio representative Dennis Kucinich. She had met him in January, while enlisting Congressional support for the Afghan Victims Fund, and had been impressed with the vision he expressed in speeches like his "Prayer for America."

He called back immediately and instead made an invitation of his own: Why not hold a press conference in Washington, DC to help galvanize Congressional opposition to war in Iraq? With the Administration still sailing on momentum from the September 11 commemorations, and with a compliant media beating the drums of war, it became clear that Congress would be voting on some form of a war resolution before, rather than after, the midterm elections—likely before the end of the month, possibly before the end of the week. Given that sense of urgency, Peaceful Tomorrows rose to the occasion. With only forty-eight hours notice, Rice, Rockefeller, Campbell, Ryan and Barry Amundson, Kelly, Lasar, and Potorti converged on the Capitol on September 25.

Standing on the steps of the House Cannon building, with the Capitol dome as a backdrop, Kucinich introduced the family members, letting them speak for themselves to the sizable press

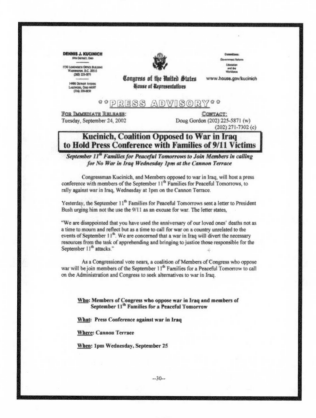

delegation. Other congresspeople flanked the family members and stayed afterwards to express their solidarity.

While the family members were adamant about stopping the use of their loved ones' deaths as an excuse to go to war with Iraq, the first question fielded at the press event was whether they would support military action if a link was determined between Saddam Hussein and Al-Qaeda. Both Condoleeza Rice and Donald Rumsfeld had recently claimed that Hussein offered Al-Qaeda members training and safe harbor inside his country's borders—begging the question of how that could be, when Islamic fundamentalists like bin Laden loathed secular Arabs in general and had contempt for Hussein in particular.

"If there is proof of this connection, we would welcome an open look at that," said Terry Rockefeller. "To our knowledge, the top Al-Qaeda members that have been captured to date have been in Pakistan, through diplomatic and intelligence channels, not through war and not through bombing. So we would like to see more of the pursuit of the people who are really responsible for September 11 through those same intelligence channels. That seems to be most effective."

In fact, more than a year after the commencement of bombing in Afghanistan, Peaceful Tomorrows' view that police work and diplomacy, not military action, would prove most effective in apprehending terrorists was wholly vindicated—as was their belief that innocent people did not have to die as "collateral damage" for those apprehensions to occur. Spain and Germany, as well as Pakistan, had delivered Al-Qaeda members without dropping a single bomb.

The group stayed on to lobby legislators against the war. Members of Peaceful Tomorrows made seventy visits to legislators to plumb their positions, finding virtually unanimous reports of phone calls running 10-, 100-, and in one district from Oregon, 400-to-1 against the war.

They spoke at rallies, vigils, and other gatherings of the emerging antiwar network around Washington, DC as groups brought their members in for a day or two of lobbying. Reinforcements, including Kat Tinley, Matthew Lasar, and new family member Scott Ephriam, would also join in a day of meetings with Senate and Congressional staffers. The group visited the Senate gallery to witness senator after senator invoking September 11 as a reason to go to war in Iraq, and heard what would be Minnesota Senator Paul Wellstone's last speech against the war in Iraq. Campbell was shocked by the timidity of both the House and Senate leadership.

"I met with Tom Daschle's staff, who assured me that he agreed with our position, but was afraid that he wouldn't have enough votes to counter the resolution authorizing war with Iraq," Campbell said. "Over and over, I met with people in leadership positions abdicating their responsibility."

Meanwhile, Kucinich and other progressives were building opposition that would result in a majority of House Democrats voting against the war. But this group would not include members of the Democratic leadership, who were busy hedging their bets in the run-up to the midterm elections.

"There was such a climate of fear in Washington," Campbell said. "There was a sniper on the loose in the suburbs, Capitol Hill was jumpy with bomb scares, and Administration officials alledged that Saddam Hussein posed an immediate threat to the United States. One staffer told me that the atmosphere was reminscent of the anthrax scares a year earlier, when the Patriot Act had been passed—they felt terrorized."

The press did its part. In TV-land, war was already a done deal, and if there were millions of Americans opposed to it, their views were rarely covered. When the occasional naysayer found his or her way into the line of fire, they were marginalized. Campbell's September 29 appearance with CNN's Wolf Blitzer was typical:

Blitzer: I'm trying to find out if you're just a pacifist or if there's a serious issue here that you're trying to consider.

Campbell: We believe that war is not the answer . . .

Blitzer: So it's basically a pacifistic position: You don't see any justification for war under any circumstances.

Campbell: I think particularly under these circumstances, a war resolution is not justified right now. I think we need to start with the UN, I think we need to start sending in weapons inspectors, seeing what happens. If they're not in compliance, come back, move it to another level. We're very concerned right now that this is being used for political ends, that they're pushing through these votes before the election, that this is not something that needs to happen right now, this needs to be carefully considered . . .

Blitzer: Three thousand people were killed on September 11, and there are thousands and thousands of family members who have suffered. You have, what, thirty to fifty people so far who have come out and supported you, which is a tiny, tiny percentage of the family members. So basically you're only representing a minute fraction of all of the victims' family members . . .

Blitzer's implication—that the "thousands and thousands" of family members not publicly supporting Peaceful Tomorrows' position therefore favored the war—was supported by zero evidence. Inexplicably, no survey polling 9/11 family members specifically on their views of the war—or, in fact, on their views of anything—had ever been taken by a news outfit, including CNN. Like the absence of a 9/11 investigation, the absence of a definitive survey of 9/11 families created a vacuum into which anyone could suggest anything—and did.

The media screaming for war, Congress ignoring its constituents, the Administration repeating undocumented accusation after undocumented accusation—indeed, October of 2002 was a genuinely odd time in Washington. It was in this climate of fear that the House and Senate voted to abdicate their Constitutional responsibilities and grant war-making power to the President. In the midterm elections that followed, the Democrats would lose their majority in the Senate.

Appearing in the President's backyard, however, did have one benefit: The Administration seemed to notice. On October 3, the group received a reply to its letter, from Condoleeza Rice. "The United States is one of many countries that is working with the United Nations to find a diplomatic solution to Saddam Hussein's continued threat to world peace and stability," she wrote. "We join you and other grieving families across America— all those who lost loved ones in the brutal terrorist attacks of September 11—in our continued hope that war will not be necessary to end Saddam's repressive leadership."

THE WHITE HOUSE

WASHINGTON

October 3, 2002

Dear Ms. Campbell:

The President asked that I express his gratitude to you and the other September Eleventh family members for sharing your views on Iraq and military preemption with him. Currently, the United States is one of many countries that is working with the United Nations to find a diplomatic solution to Saddam Hussein's continued threat to world peace and stability.

We join you and other grieving families across America -- all those who lost loved ones in the brutal terrorist attacks of September 11 -- in our continued hope that war will not be necessary to end Saddam's repressive leadership, gain Iraqi compliance with United Nations resolutions, and convince Baghdad to abandon its pursuit of weapons of mass destruction.

Saddam must now show the world that he shares our same commitment to peace. Regrettably, his decade long record of non-compliance with the rule of law and internationally accepted standards of conduct is cause for concern. His dismal record underscores why the President is committed to the belief that if diplomacy fails, America must be capable of using force to protect its national interests, basic freedoms, and way of life. Again, we hope this forceful course of action will be unnecessary, but the enduring lesson of the last century is that appeasement and accommodation are ineffective policy instruments against evil and tyranny.

We keep you and all who have suffered from the tragedy on September 11 in our thoughts and prayers.

Sincerely,

Condoleezza Rice
Assistant to the President
for National Security Affairs

Ms. Kelly Campbell
Co-Director
September Eleventh Families for a Peaceful
Tomorrow
5111 Telegraph Avenue #185
Oakland, California 94609

Never separate the lives you live from the words you speak.
—Senator Paul Wellstone

Chapter Fourteen

As Congress voted to authorize war in Iraq, "Afghan Portraits of Grief: The Civilian/Innocent Victims of U.S. Bombing in Afghanistan"—a study jointly produced by Peaceful Tomorrows and Global Exchange—achieved what many in the group had long spoken of, giving civilians in Afghanistan what had so generously been given to their own loved ones: names, faces, a recognition of their humanity. But it received scant public notice on the anniversary of the commencement of bombing in Afghanistan. Campbell participated in a quiet memorial ceremony in Northern Virginia, where the Afghan community came together to honor the dead. A far cry from the hype surrounding the September 11 commemorations, their day of mourning went virtually unnoticed in the American media.

Filmmaker Michael Moore called the group and offered them the New York premiere of his new film, *Bowling for Columbine,* to use as a fundraiser. The documentary, which focused with painful honesty on the culture of violence in America, particularly gun violence, seemed instantly to capture the zeitgeist: The Washington-area sniper remained in full rampage, and Moore acknowledged fielding daily calls from the press for his take on the current body count. A resident of New York City on 9/11, Moore admired Peaceful Tomorrows' response, and announced that his next project, tentatively entitled *Fahrenheit 9/11,* would focus on September 11 and its aftermath.

Given the gravity of the President's doctrine of pre-emption, and the inevitability of his move on Iraq, a national organization was a necessary next step for the peace movement. On October

25, the day before a major march on Washington, Potorti joined members of seventy national peace groups for an organizing meeting of what would become United for Peace and Justice. They gathered at the People for the American Way conference room—United Methodists, Black Voices for Peace, the National Youth and Student Peace Coalition, the Iraq Pledge of

David Potorti and Michael Moore at the New York premiere of Bowling for Columbine; *the film would go on to win the Academy Award for Best Documentary*

Resistance, the National Organization of Women, Friends of the Earth, Labor Against War, Veterans for Peace, Veterans for Common Sense, the AFSC, Peace Action, National Network Against the War in Iraq, MoveOn, Not in Our Name, True Majority, Sojourners, Center for Community Change, Institute for Public Accuracy, the Institute for Policy Studies, and others.

The groups hadn't even finished introducing themselves when word came of Senator Paul Wellstone's plane gone missing, and shortly afterward, the death of all on board. Progressive Wellstone was one of the few members of the Senate to oppose the Iraq war resolution, and his reelection could have determined whether control of the body remained in Democratic hands.

"It was just a horrible blow," Potorti said. "It raised the stakes exponentially, because everyone realized how close the election was going to be, and how much could be riding on the outcome. The whole room took a break. Everyone got on the phone. I got into a prayer circle in the lobby."

When they returned, the activists drafted an organizing statement for United for Peace and Justice. "The demand placed on us by world events is to deal with the Iraq crisis and to work to stop the war that is being planned," it read. "This is unfolding in a global context where other crises can, and will, erupt in connection to the Iraq crisis, and they, too, will demand our action. In addition, we will oppose new repressive measures at home. We can and will work together now, focused on stopping this war, and as we go forward we will discuss other issues and the larger context."

The march on Washington the following day was notable for its size and for the presence of signs honoring Wellstone's legacy. Voices in the Wilderness' rainbow bus was there, and Potorti happily reconnected with many of the activists he had met in the year since the Walk for Healing and Peace. In that regard, he was experiencing the same regenerative power of mass gatherings that kept everyone coming back—you might not see them on television, but they were there, together, and their power was palpable.

Still, the coverage of the march itself quickly became a bone of contention. "As a marcher, my sense was that it was as big, and most likely bigger, than April [the gathering that drew 75,000 people]," Potorti said, "but there was something really screwy about the reporting that day. The marchers always tend to overestimate, and the news always tends to underestimate—that's normal. But I remember going online that night, hours after the march had finished, and reading an Associated Press report that said that hundreds—hundreds!—had marched that day. It was so far off base that I couldn't believe it."

In fact, the march was two miles long, and drew approximately 150,000 participants. It took hours, and actually passed by the Associated Press building. But AP was not alone in its perspective. The evening of the march, NPR's *All Things Considered* tallied the marchers as numbering "fewer than ten thousand," and that turnout had disappointed the organizers. A day later—in the wake of complaints—NPR's *Weekend Edition* reported organizer's estimates of 100,000 as being more accurate. And a *New York Times* report that "thousands" of protesters were on hand, representing far fewer than expected, was corrected on October 30 to read, "[The march] drew 100,000 by police estimates and 200,000 by organizers,' forming a two-mile wall of marchers around the White House. The turnout startled even organizers, who had taken out permits for 20,000 marchers."

* * *

Whether from continuing emotional and mental fallout over 9/11, the difficulties of working over long distances and communicating largely by phone and e-mail, or from the personality conflicts that plague every family or working group, fall 2002 was also a rough patch of road for Peaceful Tomorrows. "The honeymoon's over," was how Kelly would describe it: Having done the heavy lifting of establishing the group and contributing various quantities of blood, sweat, and tears to its growth, it was now time to deal with the reality of keeping the organization in business.

"The September 11 anniversary was like an emotional marker," Kelly said, "and once the anniversary passed, there was less 'gentleness' within the group, less attention paid to feelings, and more paid to getting down to business and figuring how we would work as an organization. We were all thrown together by circumstance—it's not like I saw an ad in the newspaper for my job with Peaceful Tomorrows. The challenge became figuring out what our roles were and how we would work together. If our organization was going to survive, it was a necessity."

"It came down to expectations," Potorti said. "What was my role, and what was everyone else's? We had invented these titles for ourselves, but in reality the group functioned in a much more fluid and democratic manner. The phone would ring, with a new

Peaceful Tomorrows' first holiday card

idea from someone, or a new invitation, and we would all go running off in different directions. Sometimes we'd run too far. But everyone did whatever it took to keep things going. Personally, I had to let go of a lot of expectations about control and following protocol."

It helped to know that theirs wasn't a unique situation— other groups, forged in the aftermath of 9/11, seemed to be going through the same challenges at the same time. But their problems were largely solved by a group reality-check: of expectations, job descriptions, and directions for the future. The group would need to grow—it was time for an advisory board of family members whose participants could address money issues, organizational issues, and other big-picture items that the core staff was too busy or distracted to consider. And it was essential to meet in the flesh, another reminder of the limitations of electronic communication in capturing the nuances of human interaction.

A pre-Thanksgiving retreat in New York was planned to rethink the organization and revisit the group's mission state- ment and goals. The call for an advisory board was addressed with commitments from Bodley, Rice, and Rockefeller. It turned out to be enough to create a subtle new dynamic among the group's members and to reenergize them. Campbell and Barry Amundson created holiday cards featuring a photo donated to the group by Linda Wan: two kids wrapped in a peace flag at a September, 2001 vigil in Ann Arbor, Michigan. They divvied up names and addresses of friends and support- ers, and everyone took a stack of cards to sign and send. Before going their separate ways, Campbell invited them to form a cir- cle and hold hands. They remembered why they were doing the unique work they were doing: to honor their family members, lost on September 11. Lasar summed it up this way: "The bot- tom line is, we love each other. And we're stuck with each other."

As peace came to the group, Campbell and Barry Amundson would accept an invitation to India, to give a keynote address at the convening of the Nonviolent Peaceforce in Delhi, India, a conference attended by delegates from fifty nations. Based on the "Peace Army" that Gandhi was creating in his last days, the Nonviolent Peaceforce is working to create an international, nonviolent "army" to be deployed to avert conflicts around the world. And, perhaps as a sign of hope, the Potortis would have a daughter on December 10, International Human Rights Day.

I saw a program of your organization on tv here in Tokyo. I feel great sorrow for the state the world is in now. The United States government is mistaken if they believe that war will solve these problems. War will only cause escalation, retaliation and revenge. The events of 9/11 should not be forgotten, and if current events keep progressing, tragic events around the globe will continue and thousands of innocent people will die.

*

When I was young just 30 years ago, U.S.A used to be a paradise to me. America, where there is freedom, there are open-minded people, and great opinion leaders, and more. But after 9.11, everything has changed to me and what is worse every thought of mine about America turned to be just a fantasy.

*

I commend you for what you're doing, so long as not one of you accepted a penny of federal monies or participated in the lawsuits against our government for your losses on 9/11. You CAN NOT have it both ways.

*

You are to be commended for turning your loss into helping others. I hope that people from other countries will learn that the majority of Americans do not support war. If anyone can look at those pictures of war-torn children and not feel sad, then they are truly cold-hearted. I hope that websites like this one will spawn a world-wide movement to end all war. I firmly believe that ALL nations should disarm and destroy all weapons.

*

Hey, peace would be great. Too bad that can only happen if everyone feels the same way you do. Guess what
. . . . . . they don't! Guess how many peaceful men an evil
man can kill with a six shooter . . . ? Sorry losers,
you'll have to hope for utopia on the next level, 'cause
you ain't gettin' it here!

In our time, political speech and writing are largely the defense of the indefensible. Things like the continuance of British Rule in India, the Russian purges and deportations, the dropping of the atom bombs on Japan, can be defended, but only by arguments which are too brutal for most people to face, and which do not square with the professed aims of the political parties. Thus political language has to consist largely of euphemism, question-begging and sheer cloudy vagueness.
—George Orwell, *Politics and the English Language* (1946)

We've been warned there are evil people in this world. We've been warned so vividly. And we'll be alert. Your government is alert. The governors and mayors are alert that evil folks still lurk out there. As I said yesterday, people have declared war on America and they have made a terrible mistake. My Administration has a job to do and we're going to do it. We will rid the world of the evildoers.
—President George W. Bush (2002)

Anyone who has the power to make you believe absurdities has the power to make you commit injustices.
—Voltaire (1767)

Chapter Fifteen

Peaceful Tomorrows' delegation to Iraq—made up of Colleen Kelly, Kristina Olsen, Kathleen Tinley, and Terry Rockefeller—left New York City on January 5, 2003. They knew the trip would be controversial, perhaps the most controversial action the group had taken, but the person-to-person nature of the journey would be its focus: They would leave politics to the politicians. It was, at heart, a deeply personal decision.

"In January, I had read a newspaper piece about Derrill Bodley going to Afghanistan," said Terry Rockefeller, "and I knew that if I hadn't been mopping my parents up off the floor at the time, I would have gone if I could—it was so electric.

When the opportunity came, Iraq was a place I couldn't not go to. I had to be there. I just think we don't feel often enough that people in other places in the world are truly human beings like us. And I couldn't think of any other way to make that point more strongly. But I was scared. I had totally irrational fears about my safety. I had fears about people thinking I was nuts."

In fact, she and others in the delegation went through their e-mail address books, deciding that they should tell their friends and business associates about the trip and their reasons for taking it.

"I sent e-mails to probably two hundred people, and I was amazed that their responses were extraordinarily positive," Rockefeller said. "Overwhelmingly, they said, 'Thank you, you're doing something I wish I had the courage to do.'" She would also come to experience one of the whimsical effects of press coverage from the trip: hearing from people she hadn't been in contact with for decades.

But they knew from the earlier trips to Afghanistan that there was no way to avoid the political ramifications of the mission: They would be called naïve; unpatriotic; pawns of Saddam Hussein. These were familiar words, and cropped up in interviews and e-mails even before the delegation left the country. Still, it remained a personal journey.

"I am traveling to Iraq as a witness for peace," Kristina Olsen said. "I feel a deep sense of moral responsibility, both as a citizen of the global community, and as a person who lost a loved one on September 11, to promote the message of peace—by bearing witness to the suffering of innocent people, as well as by working toward creating an opening for constructive, nonviolent approaches to dealing with conflict in our world. This, I feel, is the most meaningful way I can honor the memory of my sister."

"My hope is that all people will come to realize that loss of more human life will not solve the problems of the world," Tinley added.

Mother, child, and Colleen Kelly at Basra Hospital, Iraq

After spending a day in Amman, Jordan, to obtain visas from the Iraqi embassy, they flew to Baghdad. The words *"Down USA"* were stenciled in red on the ramp heading into the airport—but the welcome inside, from Wadah, an Iraqi government minder, was much warmer. They would stay at the Andalus Hotel on the ancient Tigris River, which received millions of tons of sewage a day—a public sanitation disaster due to lack of machinery and parts as a result of sanctions.

Seeing the group's itinerary the next morning at breakfast, Kelly announced, "I'm going to cry all day." It would begin at the al-Mansour Pediatric Hospital, where they would see firsthand the long-lasting effects of sanctions and war, particularly the absence of the most basic medical supplies. "Sanctions," a doctor would tell them, "are the real weapons of mass destruction."

They ate lunch with a family whose historic, 100-year-old Baghdad home had been largely destroyed in the 1991 Gulf War by bombs targeting a nearby bridge. Since then, they had painstakingly reconstructed the first floor. Iraqi arts and crafts from the country's many different ethnic groups filled the rooms and were also on sale in a small gallery. Speaking perfect English, the family and their friends shared their frustrations with twelve years of sanctions, and talked of the hatred for the United States that was growing in their country.

"At least there are people who understand us," one woman said, "who know that we are victims, not aggressors . . . Unfortunately, a few people are ruining this world and spoiling it . . . We can be together, we can be happy. You can eat our food, we can talk your language. So what's wrong? Why should we fight each other? Why should we kill each other's children? Why?"

It would be a sentiment repeated throughout their stay: Before 1990, many Iraqis had looked to the United States with appreciation and respect, admiring its freedoms and democracy and sending members of their families to schools in the U.S. and Europe. To remember that friendship, only to see it disappear in the wake of the Gulf War, was a source of hurt pride and personal resentment. And the economic situation created a new kind of fear: Parents who had taken pride in the secular nature of their country were seeing their children forced to leave Iraq to find work in nations like Saudi Arabia, where they were being exposed to fundamentalist regimes.

Terry Rockefeller and Kristina Olsen in Iraq

They visited the al-Amiriya civilian bomb shelter, hit twice in succession by U.S. smart bombs on February 13, 1991, and preserved as a monument to the more than four hundred who died there. Family members whose loved ones died in the attack came to greet the delegation, sharing their stories. Staring up at the gaping hole in the ceiling, the Peaceful Tomorrows members in the delegation would remember the twisted steel of the World Trade Center, and like Rita Lasar, would observe a painful symmetry. They would see the photos of the families lost in the bombing— just as photos had been posted of their loved ones lost on September 11: a man who lost his wife and seven children; another who lost his mother, four sisters, and brother; a man who lost his wife, three daughters, and one son; a woman whose three daughters perished. Some might resist the comparison of a terrorist attack on civilians to an errant bomb. But for those on the receiving end of violence, the similarities couldn't have been clearer.

The delegation would come to know that virtually everyone they met, from civilians to their government "minder," had been touched by war or the effects of war—the Iran/Iraq war or the Gulf War—which made the impending war with the U.S. a harsh reality little-known to the typical American. "We don't want war. We want peace," said one victim. "But if war is imposed on us, we will never obey the U.S. demands or orders— U.S. or any other foreigners. Never."

A visit to a school revealed that although the building itself was a mess, the government had provided all the supplies that were needed—including computers, which arrived four years earlier. But the English teacher hosting their visit confided that she and two other teachers at the school had breast cancer, and, crying, begged the delegation to help them get medicine. Under UN sanctions, chemotherapy drugs were unavailable in Iraq— they were considered "dual-use" items which could allegedly be used as chemical weapons.

It was in Basra that the delegation got a taste of life in the southern no-fly zone that was bombed almost daily by Allied forces since the end of the Gulf War. "As we walked from home to home, this crowd of children came out of the woodwork and followed us around like we were the pied piper," Kelly said. "When we were going back to our minibus, the air-raid sirens went off. All of us flinched and looked around, trying to see if there was a bomb shelter. But to the children, it meant nothing— they were desensitized to the chronic sound of the sirens. I remember getting on the bus and thinking, the day is going to come, and soon, when these air raid sirens are going to be real, and these children will not seek shelter. There was the realization of what it means to live with violence every day—in order to survive psychologically, you have to turn yourself off, because you can't live constantly on high-alert. I thought about the color-coded alerts from the Department of Homeland Security—how does a nation live like that? It burns out your warning system."

Members of Peaceful Tomorrows hold a banner during a vigil in Baghdad

You should feel ashamed to call yourself American. The people of Aphganastan are no longer living under an oppressive regime that fosters and promotes terrorist activities. The coming war in Iraq is lesser of two evils and although it saddens me that good people will lose there lives in this conflict it gives me hope that my family, your family and innocent families in the region will be able to breath a sigh of relief that governments like the Taliban and Baath Party of Iraq will no longer be capable of providing the means and wherewithal to terrorize and murder innocent people in our country.

*

By not supporting your country and not supporting the war against Saddam, you indirectly support a bloodthirsty killer named Saddam Hussein. YOu all make me sick. I believe that the ones who started this peace bullshit were all overaged hippy losers who burnt themselves out in the 60s. Ever since the end of the Vietnam War, you've been searching for a reason to bring back your peace movement so you can call off work delivering pizzas to join a protest and get high. You all need to get a life. Just do some real research and find out what you really suppport. Or you can move to Iraq so you can be closer to your buddy, Saddam Hussein. Fucking traitors!!!!

*

The supporters of terrorism that created this site should be ashamed to call themselves Americans, if they even are Americans. Of all people, victims of the Sep.11, 2001 terrorist attacks in lower Manhattan and the DC area should be supporting the elimination of the greatest threat to the future of the United States and our brothers and sisters in Israel: ISLAM. Of course, Saddam and his billions of allies in the Islamic world, as well as France, Russia, China, and Iraq's other allies, is not the only threat to the U.S. North Korea must be pursued as well.

*

In Oklahoma City, where I live, more and more people are expressing their support for disarmament to be achieved through peaceful methods. We have a saying here: "In Oklahoma, we know that one bomb is too many."

*

I was amazed to see on the Omaha, Nebraska 10 P.M. news Friday evening January 24 that some American members of your organization had actually visited Iraq, critizing America and its approach to the Iraqui regime and its terrorist goals. Like Jane Fonda visiting VietNam (to criticise the American Forces) decades ago . . . how un-patriotic . . . to think of the thousands of Americans who have fought and died for this country over the years, just so your organization could visit terrorist governments like the one in Iraq. Why not move over there and try protesting ? It is only because you live in the United States Of America that you are allowed to visit terrorist countries and live to complain for another day. I am very disappointed . . .

*

To all you misguided people who want revenge and retaliation against the people who 'hate' your country: do you ever wonder why you are 'hated'? It's high time you start respecting other cultures and countries. Change your attitudes and stop believing you are this and you are that. We are all the same regardless of our country

of birth, culture etc. As someone else put it, stop talking so much and start listening more. We live on planet
earth, not planet America. Be fair and respectful and
giving, and it shall be returned to you. The events of
9/11 were horrible, but stop using them as an excuse
for revenge. The memories of the people who died would
be better off used for peace.

No man is an island, entire of itself; every man is a piece
of the continent, a part of the main. The death of one
diminishes all. For all are bound together in the
bundle of life. We are involved in Mankind.
—John Donne, from *Devoting*

Chapter Sixteen

"It was incredibly personally validating," Rockefeller said of her trip to Iraq. "It gave me confidence that, people-to-people, you can make a difference. Our delegation was covered by the Al-Jazeera network, and here I am, an experienced journalist, thinking, 'Oh my god, I'm being covered by the enemy.' And then I realized that the reporter really was interested in the things I wanted her to be—why did you come, what did you learn, why are you opposed to war, what do you think the chances are that the antiwar movement will succeed? When she showed up again the next day, I realized that they were really interested in us, that we mattered to them, and that they thought we mattered to their audience."

But if Peaceful Tomorows' person-to-person delegation to Iraq was successful in terms of forging links among colleagues and victims of terrorism and war, as well as highlighting the complexities of history and international relations, those complexities were in short supply in official discourse following their return to the United States.

Twenty-four hours after their return, on January 15, 2003—the calendar birthday of Reverend Martin Luther King, Jr.—members of the delegation would appear on the highly rated *Connie Chung* show. It was a curious mix of welcome media attention and government cheerleading. Chung would cut off each respondent's legs at the same time she invited them to run with a question:

Kristina, some people would think what you have done is not only bold, but they might even call it unpatriotic. Can you explain your mission?

. . . But you weren't allowed to go just anywhere you wanted to go, right? I think that, by having handlers or guides or escorts, that people would say, well, you were just pawns of President Saddam Hussein.

. . . You know what, Terry? Some people might say, well, that's naïve of you to think that the people could actually carry on some kind of dialogue, because Saddam Hussein is so oppressive.

As the family members spoke, onscreen graphics read, *"Iraqi Government Shepherded 9/11 Kin"* and, *"Other 9/11 Kin Back U.S. Policy on Iraq."* Call it covering their bases or legitimate journalism, it was another reflection of the strange state of American media in the run-up to war.

"The frustration comes when I don't have the right forum to actually engage these people," Rockefeller said. "I did a horrible AM talk radio show in Florida when we got back from Iraq, and I was sitting there thinking there is something terribly sad about America that people find it entertaining that this host wants to bait me. But I had gotten the notion that I was going to try and make the interview work. I emphasized that our troops would be killed if we went to war, about the extraordinary expense of sending our army around the world, how the weapons inspectors were being effective, and how it was much less expensive to keep them there than to go to war. He stopped and said, 'Now, you're not going to let money be the deciding issue? How much would it be worth to have your sister back?' I took a deep breath and said I wouldn't even dignify an insulting question like that with an attempt at an answer. Afterwards, I felt like doing the interview wasn't worth the emotional price, because I probably didn't change much. I would love to know that I made an impact."

Colleen Kelly was one of five people—the others included a U.S. serviceman, an Iraqi schoolteacher, an Israeli citizen, and an Iraqi exile living in the U.S.—profiled on a *Dateline* NBC special, *The Road to Baghdad,* hosted by Tom Brokaw. It would be perhaps the highest profile yet given to a member of Peaceful Tomorrows, and it would air while Kelly was in Iraq. The viewpoint of the program became clear as images of Saddam's goose-stepping troops were shown as evidence of a militarism that, in reality, posed no threat to the continental United States in the year 2003. Kelly and the Iraqi schoolteacher were the only ones who expressed reservations about the need for war.

In fact, her participation in the program had been taking place over several months and had culminated in the interview with Brokaw himself. But what prepared her for that moment was an interview she did, only hours before her rendezvous with NBC, with an independent Australian documentarian.

"He had been born in the former Yugoslavia, grew up without a father, lost his mother to suicide in an Australian refugee camp, and had been shot three times in the leg," Kelly said. "He really went after me about my position on nonviolence—when mass genocide is happening, how can you say the Air Force shouldn't be sent in? He made me think very hard about these issues, because he had such intense experiences. As much as I believe in nonviolence, looking at Rwanda, or the Balkans, when there is mass slaughter of civilians, isn't that a time when war is necessary? My answer was, how can we help create a world where that response is not necessary? And it made me think about how ridiculous our premise was for going into Iraq now— why didn't we go there in the 1980s when they were gassing their own people?"

THE TRANSFORMING POWER OF MUSIC
by *Kristina Olsen*

My sister, Laurie, lived in Los Angeles, but in the days before September 11 she flew with her daughter back to our childhood home in Massachusetts to help our elderly mother move. I am grateful for the time we had together for those few days. We joked and laughed and sang silly songs from our childhood, reminiscing about some of our old antics. On Monday night we hugged each other goodbye. I told my sister that I loved her. The last thing she said to me was, "I love Kristina's hugs, she gives such good hugs!" That was the last time I saw her.

After the tragic events of that day, my niece Francisca, who was flying west on a different flight, told me about having a "slumber party" with her mom the night before. They shared a bedroom at my sister Lyra's house, and talked about things they had never talked about before: the endlessness of the cosmos, other life-forms in the universe, and, for some reason, the subject of war. Laurie said, "I don't believe in war. I think it's wrong to send young people off to fight, to kill or be killed, because of a policy."

My sister was a gentle person with a pure and loving heart. One of the traits I so admired about Laurie was that she never said a bad word about anyone. There was nothing more important to my sister than family. She worked full-time at home as a medical transcriber, building up her own clientele after years of working in Los Angeles hospitals. When her grandaughter, Amanda, was born, Laurie took care of her in her own home, five days a week, eight hours a day, for the first six months of her life, so she wouldn't have to go into day care.

Even though my sister and I lived three thousand miles apart and couldn't see each other very frequently, we shared a special closeness and friendship that is reflected in a poem that I wrote for one of her birthdays:

My sister is a friend for life
We share a common past.
The weaving of our childhood dreams,
These threads will always last.

Toboganning down snowy hills
And walks on Fenno drive;
Clanging pots and pans to Mitch (Miller),
Hot cocoa before the fire.

Christmastime with buckles sweet (a Norwegian cookie)
And springtime plum tree flowers,
These memories carry us along
To comfort in dark hours.

My sister is a friend for life,
We share a common past.
The weaving of our childhood dreams
Of Love will always last.

For the first six months following her death, I was unable to work as a nurse in the capacity of caregiver. In the acute stages of my grief at the time, I found solace and comfort in the love of family, friends, community, and most of all, in my music. It became clear to me while singing at an outdoor festival on September 15 that I would need to commit myself to the music that I had been given in order to send the message of love, understanding, and hope to the world, to help bring healing and peace to other people's hearts as well as my own. I remember how this knowing had washed over me that day, that I was being called to do this in Laurie's memory because she had embodied all of these elements of love and understanding in her own life. She had lived them, and now I was reflecting them back to the world through music sung in her memory.

When it became clear that our country's reaction to September 11 would take the form of war and further violence, the sadness and loss that my family and I were experiencing was magnified by the knowledge that other innocent people would be experiencing this same suffering. The thought that my sister's death was being used to justify further violence and suffering was too much for me to bear. So I began singing at peace vigils and gatherings, and I spoke out publicly against the war for the first time in December 2001, in an interview on a local radio station. I voiced my concern for the innocent Afghan people who were suffering and dying as a result of the U.S.-led bombing campaign that had begun in October.

I joined Peaceful Tomorrows in April of 2002 after meeting the founding members in Washington, DC. I felt an immediate connection with these people, a bond that transcended any words, as result of our common suffering. We are a family, brought together by a tragedy that took from all of us someone very precious. And as a family, we share unconditional love as well as many challenges and differences of opinion. Because of the openness and receptivity that we have toward one another and the nuances that each individual brings to the group, there is plenty of room for these differences to exist in a way that enhances, rather than detracts, from our mission and purpose. We share a willingness to listen to one another and to remain receptive to constructive feedback and ideas, which, unlike any group I have ever been a part of, allows for a workable flow.

I traveled to Afghanistan to meet with Afghan family members who had lost loved ones in the recent bombing, to listen to their stories, and to learn what life is actually like for these people, who we know so very little about.

I was shocked and humbled by the extent of their suffering, and their unabashed enthusiasm and love toward us, in spite of what they had been through. Everywhere we went in Kabul, we were greeted with dazzling smiles, open arms and hearts. One of the most deeply meaningful experiences was a memorial service for the people killed in the bombing campaign. It was attended by 125 Afghan family members and included men, women, and children of all ages. My fellow delegates, representing the Christian, Jewish, and Muslim faiths, constructed a makeshift altar in the courtyard where the service was held. It was made of colorful scarves, flowers, rubble from the bombing, and a picture of my sister Laurie, which later became a source of great interest and curiosity.

An elderly and blind Afghan gentleman sang passages from the Quran. His voice was rich and soulful, and his singing touched me so deeply that I wept, hearing the collective suffering that it seemed to embody in that moment. I was asked to sing and I shared a song called "Wherever You Go," which would become a sort of theme song for our trip:

Wherever you go, I shall go.
Wherever you live, so shall I live.
Your people will be my people
And your god will be my god too.

Wherever you go, I shall go.
Wherever you live, so shall I live.
We shall be together forever
And our love will be the gift of our lives.

The song was written by a Benedictine Monk named Gregory Norbet, and the lyrics are based, in part, on words from the Bible's Book of Ruth. When I first heard it, I remember how healing it was, and how it touched the core of my heart and released a river of tears from deep inside of me. It was sung at my sister's funeral.

After heartfelt prayers were offered and the service came to an end, a group of women gathered, expressing a desire to see my sister's picture. I watched their expressions as they examined Laurie's photograph. Tears welled up in one woman's eyes and she said to me, "I'm sorry for your sister. I know how you feel, I lost four members of my family." Then I felt a tap on my shoulder. I turned around and found a group of men who wanted to see the picture as well. One kept shaking his head, and with tears in his eyes, he expressed how sorry he was for the loss of my sister. He had lost ten family members to the bombing, and he, too, knew what it was like.

In fact, many of the Afghan people present at the memorial service had lost multiple family members in the bombing. One eight-year-old girl, Amena, had lost sixteen extended family members: her mother, her brothers and sisters, cousins, aunts, and uncles. One uncle survived, along with her father, but because of severe kidney damage, he wasn't expected to live for very long. As she spoke openly about her inconceivable trauma and the scars it left behind, she seemed more like an old woman than an eight-year-old child.

It was only after my return home to the United States that the horror of what that experience must have been like for her actually hit me on an emotional level. I knew that her suffering, and by and large the suffering of most of the people that we met in Afghanistan, was far greater than my own.

When it became clear that Iraq would be considered next in line for military intervention, I felt a deep sense of responsibility to do everything in my power to prevent it from happening. I called and faxed every member of the Senate Foreign Relations Committee, expressing my desire for restraint and time to let the inspections work. As a person who had lost someone on September 11, I expressed my feeling that waging war would not make us any safer, and would in fact increase the likelihood of future terrorist attacks on our own soil. Most importantly, I expressed the fact that I did not want my sister's death to be used to perpetuate further suffering and violence.

On our visit to Iraq, as in Afghanistan, the people welcomed us with open arms and open hearts, and treated us as honored guests despite the military attack threatened at the time. Everywhere we went, people expressed a deep desire for peace, and we encountered little hostility. Once, when we were stopped in traffic in our van, people in the surrounding vehicles stared intensely at us. I turned toward the car to my left, where a young man was staring with an angry look on his face, and flashed the universal peace sign and a smile. He was immediately transformed, and gave me a "thumbs-up" along with a dazzling smile!

The Iraqis could be very generous with their smiles, but behind the smiles was a deep sense of sadness and fear. Our visit to the al-Amiriya bomb shelter was one of the most deeply painful and meaningful experiences for me. We gathered inside this place, where the outlines of charred bodies could still be seen on the cold concrete floor, as family members recounted what had happened to their loved ones. One man described, in agonizing detail, how he had brought his wife and five children to al-Amiriya, thinking they would be safe. It was painful and difficult to listen to him, and I had to remember my reason for going to Iraq, to bear witness to the suffering of others—part of bearing witness is listening deeply to other people.

When he finished sharing his grief and venting his anger, I asked if I could sing "Path of Peace," a song I had written six months earlier, a time when I was feeling particularly sad about the violent course our country had taken. When I was finished singing, this man, understandably and vocally angry, came up to me with tears in his eyes and his hand on his heart and said, over and over again, "Thank you. Thank you. Thank you." He offered to carry my guitar for me and invited me to his home to meet the rest of his family. This healing and transformation speaks to the power of staying present and listening to one another, and to the healing power of music, the universal language of the heart.

In Basra, we visited the family of Jamil Fedah, killed by an errant U.S. bomb in the no-fly zone a month before. Upon entering the house, I was taken by the hand by one of Jamil's daughters, Sahar, and whisked into the room where her mother, Ikbal, sat draped in her black *abaya*, flanked by several female relatives. She introduced me to her mother, and as I crouched down, taking Ikbal's hands in mine, I could feel her trembling. She began to sob. I had tears, too, and said, "I'm so sorry. I'm so sorry."

Beyond those few words, there was an unspoken understanding of our mutual suffering. Even though the specific circumstances of our loved ones' deaths were different, it felt the same. Later, Sahar and I sat together on the sofa facing her mother. I asked if we could sing them a special song, but wondered if it would be allowed during the mourning period. Sahar assured me that her mother really wanted us to sing and that it was perfectly all right.

We sang "Wherever You Go," and when I looked into Sahar's eyes, tears began streaming down her face. As we left, Sahar looked at me and said, "Kristina, I loved you the moment I saw you." There was an instant and deep connection between us, and I'll carry it with me in my heart and soul, always.

I believe that we have to be able to create peace in our own lives and hearts before we can hope to have peace in the world. When we listen to one another without judging, when we listen with patience and tolerance, when we speak truthfully, with a tone of voice that promotes understanding, then we are all peacemakers, capable of healing and transforming the world we all share.

Hi, my name is Britney and i'm 16 years old. I knew i few people that died in 9/11 and people that almost died. Even if somthing like that was to happen agein i dont think that the right way to respond is going to war because if we send out the message of hate we are becoming just like them and thats what their objective was. So people speaking as someone who is going to live in the country for awhile longer, spread Peace not war, spread love not hate. PEACE . . .)

*

All my compassion and love for you courageous people of America families' victims of September 2001. Never let somebody say that french people is anti-american . most french people like most west european people are so grateful for the help brought by the american people in critical situations. Nevertheless if there is fighting between France and America it's against a politic of wild domination not to say HEGEMONY lead by Bush and the powerful lobbies. This politic is a suicid for the all planet but especially for America.

*

Nothing can ever make right what you have lost. The people of the world's thoughts are with you every day. As a British person against this unjust war, I was discussing the situation with somebody who did not share my views the other day. This person said something along the lines of "People seem to have forgotten September 11 rather quickly" as a justification for war with Iraq. This just made me so angry. Of course we haven't forgotten, but as you & I know the two incidents are not and should not be related, and the atrocity that has occured can never justify the mindless killing of thousands of other innocent people. It finding sites like yours that restores my faith in humanity.

*

I`m 12 and come from Germany. I can´t speak very good English but I understand some words. I find peaceful tomorrows good. In our school we speak over it. I see you in the TV and now I am on your homepage.

*When evil men plot, good men must plan. When evil men
burn and bomb, good men must build and bind. When
evil men shout ugly words of hatred, good men must
commit themselves to the glories of love. Where evil men
would seek to perpetuate an unjust status quo, good men
must seek to bring into a being a real order of justice.*
—Reverend Martin Luther King, Jr.

Chapter Seventeen

The Iraq delegation, like all of Peaceful Tomorrows' publicly
reported activities, had a welcome effect on recruiting new members. As the new year began, many new participants indeed took
the opportunity to join the group.

Andrea LeBlanc, a New Hampshire veterinarian who had
lost her husband, Bob, on United Airlines flight 175, shared the
same reaction to her loss that others in the group had experienced. A week after September 11, her daughter Nissa got up in
front of seven hundred people at her husband's memorial service
and said she knew for a fact that her dad would not want another person to die because of this. "After the memorial service, there
wasn't one angry word from my kids, from relatives, from friends,
there wasn't a single vengeful remark," LeBlanc said. "The focus
was all on Bob, not on how it happened."

LeBlanc had heard about the delegation to Afghanistan in
January. But it wasn't until the end of December 2002 that a
friend asked, "You do know about Peaceful Tomorrows, don't
you?" She didn't. So she introduced herself in an e-mail.

"My husband taught Cultural/Human Geography at the
University of New Hampshire for thirty-five years," she wrote.
"He believed fervently in the need for all of us to try to understand other cultures, because in such understanding there is the
undeniability of our common humanity. It is ironic that he

would be the victim of exactly opposite forces. Were he alive, he would be one of the people able to help explain how this could, and did, happen."

She was asked to join the group for the January 18 gathering and march in Washington, DC, and made plans to do so. She was also invited to meet members of the group at a press conference marking the return of the Iraq delegation. LeBlanc didn't feel like spending even more time away from home, but changed her mind after watching Colleen Kelly's appearance on *The Road to Baghdad* three days before. She had watched virtually no television since September 11, but heard about the show through an e-mail alert from Peaceful Tomorrows.

LeBlanc came into town and hung out from morning till night, joining the group for lunch on the fly, hanging out while the delegation went from media appearance to media appearance. Hearing a "report back from Iraq" that evening at the Park Slope United Methodist Church, reprising the role of Amy Goodman as emcee, she learned that September 11 family members could do more than stew in anger, accept the government at its word, or remain depressed: There could be a kind of joy in their fellowship. "It gave me the courage to do what I feel responsible to do," she said. Three days later, she traveled to Washington, DC to join Peaceful Tomorrows at the first major peace rally she had ever attended.

Adele Welty of Queens, New York lost her son, Timmy, a 34-year-old firefighter and father of two, whose rescue squad was one of the first to reach the World Trade Center. She came across a Peaceful Tomorrows link while searching the Internet for groups against the war in Iraq.

Welty wasn't getting all she needed from firefighters'-families groups, which like other 9/11 groups tended to focus on important issues of compensation and the World Trade Center memorial rather than taking official stands on issues of war and peace.

Her two other sons supported the President, her daughter opposed the war, and Timothy's widow was undecided. In January of 2003, fifteen months after her son's death, what Welty decided she needed was to take a stand against the war. She found in Peaceful Tomorrows an opportunity to do so from within the safety and comfort of a group of like-minded individuals.

Bob McIlvaine, a teacher at a critical-care psychiatric hospital, lost his son, Bobby, a Merrill Lynch executive assigned to set up a meeting at the World Trade Center—where he didn't work—on September 11. He was 26 years old and had planned to give his fiancée a ring the following weekend. His father wound up giving her the ring, and had been speaking out from day one against the direction the Bush Administration was taking the country in his son's name.

"From the very beginning, from September 11 on, it's been a matter of wanting to make a difference," McIlvaine said. "It's constantly burning inside of me: Why is this all happening? I'm trying to find some meaning out of this whole screwy thing." He met members of Peaceful Tomorrows at the *Bowling for Columbine* premiere but didn't have the opportunity to march with the group until January.

Andrew Rice, serving as membership coordinator at the time, made contact with them and others, including Catherine Montano, inviting them to join Peaceful Tomorrows at the January 18 gathering in Washington, DC. Since the vote on the war resolution the previous fall, every day held the possibility that military action could begin in Iraq. This gathering was regarded as, at the very least, one of the last opportunities for mass protest, and it drew hundreds of thousands on a bitterly cold Saturday which marked the beginning of Martin Luther King, Jr.'s birthday weekend. "It was the first time I felt like doing something," admitted Welty. "I'm not sure why, I just wasn't really functioning for a long time."

Andrew Rice marches on Washington, January 2002

"I felt an easier connection with Peaceful Tomorrows people than with the general run-of-the mill person out there carrying signs," LeBlanc said. "Sometimes it takes too much effort to talk about the personal part of it, how it's affected your life."

Members zeroed in on each other with the help of cell phones, and met under a *"Peaceful Tomorrows for All"* banner that had been carried back from Iraq. The gathering would prove to be as empowering as it was therapeutic. For new members, it was their first public action since September 11. For others, who had been members for months, it was their first opportunity to meet the people they had been e-mailing and speaking with on the phone. And for longer-term members like Rice, Bodley, and Rupp, it was a chance to recharge their batteries with new friendships. While a powerful organizing tool, the Internet could only go so far in cementing relationships.

"Face to face, people could see the other people who had been around longer, and realize that there were exciting ways of getting involved," Rice said. "It was also a time when some of them, I could tell, were ready to act—they had wanted to, but perhaps because of grief or other fears, they were not ready until now. And because of the antiwar momentum throughout the

Peaceful Tomorrows members Derrill Bodley, Eva Rupp, Helen and Bob McIlvaine, and Dana Horning march on Washington, January 2002

nation, they felt like they were ready to stand up and voice their opinions. You could tell it was a turning point for them, just as similar first-time opportunities to reject violence in my brother's name had been for me."

"I had been speaking and writing about my views, and what I knew would have been Bob's views as well, to friends and family, where I felt they were understood and accepted," LeBlanc said. "But I felt very much alone except for those close to me, and also very sad and dispirited, not at all brave or courageous. Meeting members of Peaceful Tomorrows gave me hope and courage. I felt connected to all of them, not only because of our shared losses, but because of a shared conviction that we have a responsibility to take our sorrow and help change the course of events toward a more sane and peaceful world."

In fact, the *Washington Post* would use LeBlanc's observation—that the march made her feel like she was in "a river of peaceful people"—as a story's headline about the events of the day.

"It was a lot of people who had felt really alone in their political view, having lost someone, but who had finally met a group of people who they resonated with," Rupp said. "It was powerful, meeting people who had been up till then sort of depressed with the way politics were happening. It was huge march, and it had a very huge message against the war in Iraq."

As the march wound down, the family members made a circle and held hands, each taking a moment to reflect on their feelings about the day, sharing as no others can the unique sense of grief borne by September 11 families. For Andrea LeBlanc, it didn't stop there.

"Because of being more public, and because of the newspaper articles that appeared, I said to myself, 'Well, if I believe this, I've got to do something about it,'" she recalled. She bought some boards, two feet by three feet in size, and "in a frenzy of decision- and activity-making," made them into signs and put them by the side of the road outside her house.

"The first said, '9/11 Family Against War,' and I thought, that's really negative," LeBlanc said. "So I put up another one that said, '9/11 Family for Peace.' Everybody who goes by sees them, and people are very aware of them. People will see me and come up, almost whispering that they're glad about what I said in the newspaper, or they're glad that the signs are there. And it's so odd to me—why are they so quiet about it? It's okay, you can talk out loud! As a result, I've been made aware of a lot of people around here who are of like minds, when before, I didn't know their stand. And that brought me into a bigger circle."

"I think people are starting to understand, if you sit down with them and talk with them, but it has to be one person at a time," McIlvaine said. "Anyone I talk to, they're going to have to hear the lecture if they bring up the war. I have a sign up in front of my house—'Say no to war in Iraq'—and it's been tough. I live in a suburban neighborhood, and everyone that was against the war is dropping off, I haven't heard from them, and I've still got the sign out there. Someone will go by and say, 'You're a fucking asshole.' If I could talk with that person for five minutes, there's no way they could disagree with me. One guy actually stopped and said, 'Could you please tell me why you're against the war?' and I explained it to him, and he said, 'You've got a great point.' So you never know, you've just got to keep doing it. That person might be the one who gets the word out somewhere."

* * *

A month later, Peaceful Tomorrows would get the word out at the February 15 "The World Says No to War" rally—the first major demonstration coordinated under the banner of United for Peace and Justice—that would also prove to be the last major protest before the war began. The day before, the group held a bittersweet commemoration of its first anniversary. Speakers and singers, some old friends and new, gathered at Judson Memorial Church, a historic peace church off Washington Square Park in New York City, to join in. Judson's Peter Laarman introduced the event, and the ubiquitous Amy Goodman served as emcee.

Speakers included National Council of Churches' Bob Edgar, Military Families Speak Out's Charley Richardson and Nancy Lessin, the Institute for Policy Studies' Phyllis Bennis, FOR's Janet Chisholm, and Voices in the Wilderness' Father Simon Harak. Adrienne Leban, a New York artist with the Lifework Studio, created "peace mandalas" for the group and displayed them throughout the space. Musicians included Stephan Smith, Joyce Katzberg, Bill Harley, J.C. Hopkins, Rozz Nash, Imani Uzuri, the Musician's Alliance for Peace, and Derrill Bodley. It was an evening of joyful commemoration, topped off with flowers for Goodman—a gesture of thanks for her support.

The following day began with a breakfast gathering at the

Democracy Now's Amy Goodman receives Valentine's Day flowers from Rita Lasar

UN Church Center where they had announced their group a year earlier. Kristina Olsen sang and Dan Jones performed rituals to introduce the family members to each other.

"In order to establish commonalities and to give time for 'face rites'—a term many native cultures use to define the time in a meeting when members get to tell their stories—I planned an activity in which members would have to answer a series of questions and make some kind of body movement," Jones said. He

Peaceful Tomorrows family breakfast, February 15, 2003.

asked them to put their hands on the shoulder of the first Peaceful Tomorrows member they had met.

"As the group moved to do this, I stood on a chair to see the connections," Jones said. "It was an awesome sight. Everyone, either directly or through the person they selected, was connected to a group of six people who all were selecting each other in the middle. From above, it looked like a hurricane with David,

Beverly Eckert joined the rally on February 15, her husband's birthday.

Colleen, Rita, Kelly, Barry, and Ryan in the middle. Those six were all connected to each other, too. It was remarkable to see such cohesiveness. It showed that although we didn't know specifics, we were indeed strongly connected already by the events of September 11."

As they grew to know more about each other, participants were asked to self-identify who and where they had lost someone that day—father, mother, spouse, or sibling.

"As people stepped in the center, I asked them to state the name of their lost loved one," Jones said. "The rest of us responded, *'¡Presente!'* This response comes from Latino culture, and acknowledges the continued presence of those who have died. In this way, we named those who brought us there, whose presence filled the room with us, and in whose name we wanted to resist violence."

In a short amount of time, and without a lot of talking, they were able to share an incredible amount with each other—verbally and symbolically. "After seeing the tight spiral of the 'hurricane' as people put their hands on each other's shoulders, we were able to leave the breakfast experiencing the calm 'eye' we can become at the center of the storm of violence around us," Jones said. "Much of what has been instructive to me since September 11 is the connection I feel to others around the world who have suffered violence and who continued to be threatened. The breakfast that morning allowed me to make that connection in a much more personal and intimate way."

There was little intimacy about the events that followed. As the group emerged onto the frigid streets of New York City, they joined thousands who had planned to rally and march against the war in Iraq, linked to worldwide protests with a single theme: The world says no to war. Organizers had agreed unanimously that Peaceful Tomorrows should lead the march.

Richie Havens sings "Freedom" at February 15 rally

There was only one problem: The New York City police department refused to grant a march permit. The planned route would pass the United Nations, and law enforcement was concerned with the possibility of disorder and violence. Ultimately, a rally but not a march had been approved at the final hour, with participants safely confined in "pens," or low fences, which would be closed off, block by block, as they were filled. With Homeland Security Chief Tom Ridge declaring an "orange alert," and creating a run on duct tape—actions that seemed to have more to do with protecting the Administration from criticism than protecting the country from terrorism—the police were required to be massively security-conscious and, as a result, on edge.

Derrill Bodley had been chosen to speak, and due to space concerns, only a few family members—Bodley's wife, Nancy Magnum, Catherine Montano, Andrew Rice, Ryan Amundson, and Beverly Eckert (whose lost husband, Sean Rooney, had been born on February 15)—could join him to represent the group onstage. As they were ushered backstage, the rest of the Peaceful Tomorrows delegation—like tens of thousands of other protesters—found themselves in a uniquely frustrating position of being herded farther and farther north up First Avenue away from the stage: "Pens" had been filled, and closed, leaving the only remaining open space a greater and greater distance away.

"I don't know how many street festivals I went to when I lived in New York," Potorti said, "but I remember all of them—even the ones that drew a million people over the course of a weekend—being open, relaxed, and somewhat fun. You could come and go as you pleased. But on February 15, getting herded into one of these pens and having that energy confined in an artificial space really raised the tension level. There were police in riot gear and on horseback, and they were totally unnecessary—

this was a peace rally. They created way more problems than they solved."

It was while the family members were inside a pen that word came via cell phone that the group, in force, was now being requested to appear onstage during Bodley's remarks. Led by Colleen Kelly's six-year-old daughter, as many of them as possible held hands and snaked through the crowd. Reaching a barrier, they convinced a police officer that they were needed onstage, and were allowed to climb over the fence—allowing the 71-year-old Lasar to impress her son, Raphael, and granddaughter, Emma, with her determined agility. When others in the crowd began to storm the barricades, testing the officer's generosity, only about a third of the Peaceful Tomorrows delegation managed to claw its way to the stage. But for those who did, it was a powerful experience to hear Derrill Bodley insist, "We have the

Peaceful Tomorrows members Kelly Campbell, Adele Welty, Andrew Rice, Kristina Olsen, Cat Allision, Ryan Amundson, and Apple Newman at February 15 rally

capacity, as Americans and human beings, to produce the materiels of peace instead of war. We have the knowledge and resources, the tools of understanding, respect, and love, to build—in our own minds, in our own nation, and in the world—a culture of peace achieved through peaceful means."

As the protesters gathered together, as many as 500,000 strong, to hear speakers and performers including Desmond Tutu, Pete Seeger, Harry Belafonte, Danny Glover, Julian Bond, Phyllis Bennis, Susan Sarandon, and Welfare Poets, and to hear Richie Havens sing "Freedom," it seemed, on that freezing day, like it might be possible to get some.

* * *

Meanwhile, on the other side of the world in the African nation of Guinea—a ninety-five-percent Muslim country—Eva Rupp was doing refugee interviews for her staff job with the new Office of Homeland Security, and was watching the events on television.

"The main TV stations that we got were Al-Jazeera, Lebanese Broadcasting, Middle Eastern Broadcasting, Abu Dhabi TV, and the BBC," she said. "The news, all day long, was about the protests—not just the New York protests, but protests all over Europe as well as in Singapore, Indonesia, and Egypt, where protests are illegal. In Nigeria, where the Christians and Muslims have committed so many horrible atrocities against each other, they were marching together in the streets against the war. What was interesting to me were the protests in the developing countries, where people didn't have enough to eat, but were still taking to the streets against the war." In fact, there were antiwar protests in six hundred towns and cities around the world that day.

In New York, as the family members looked out over the crowd lining First Avenue—and heard reports that protesters were so numerous that they had effectively shut down several avenues to the west—they realized that they were part of a powerful force, one that could not be contained by freezing weather, police barricades, or color-coded alerts. Indeed, even the media had to take notice.

The following day, *New York Newsday* featured pictures of protests from around the world with the headline, *"Mass Appeal: Millions Around the World Rally Against War in Iraq."* The *New York Times*, which like so much of the U.S. media had been slow to recognize the antiwar movement, noted in an article by Patrick Tyler, "The huge antiwar demonstrations around the world this weekend are reminders that there may still be two superpowers on the planet: the United States and world public opinion."

Marching and becoming active is a way of validating
Timmy's life, and giving meaning to his death—helping
other people, which is what he was living to do. And if I
can do that through Peaceful Tomorrows—because I'm
not the kind of person who's going to go out on my
own—it helps me to feel that Timmy's presence on this
earth is being validated. If I can help other people to sur-
vive or have a better life as a result of our efforts against
violence, then that's someting I can do in his name.
—Adele Welty, Peaceful Tomorrows

Chapter Eighteen

While millions in the U.S. and around the world marched against the war on the weekend of February 15, President Bush rejected the idea that the protests could affect his decision to invade Iraq, likening such a course to using "focus groups" to determine foreign policy. In the face of such gross marginalization of American citizens, and lack of respect for "the opinions of mankind," a United for Peace and Justice (UFPJ) meeting was held in Washington on the second weekend of March, where activists explored how to take protest to the next level. With troop deployments now at sufficient levels for a ground invasion, it became clear that the other shoe was about to drop.

A weeklong campaign of civil disobedience was proposed, and Campbell, who had been in town to speak at Congresswoman Eddie Bernice Johnson's annual World of Women for World Peace Breakfast, commemorating International Women's Day, decided that she would commit to the action. It was something the group had discussed since the previous fall, but they had never found an appropriate venue for "putting their bodies on the line." Now the stakes were sufficiently raised, and if there was little time to properly organize the action, there was sufficient commitment to make it happen.

Under the umbrella of UFPJ, a press conference was held on the Capitol steps, kicking off the call for a week of nonviolent civil disobedience against the war in an effort to "take back the Capitol." Speakers included Military Families Speak Out cofounder Nancy Lessin, whose stepson was a marine deployed in the Gulf; Bob Edgar, general secretary of the National Council

*Peaceful Tomorrows members Adele Welty, Rita Lasar,
and Bob McIlvaine prepare for march to the Capitol*

of Churches; UFPJ's Bob Wing; Molly McGrath, representing the National Student and Youth Coalition; Congressman Jim McDermott; Reverend Graylan Hagler; and a local Iraqi-American family.

There was a slight hitch: Several visiting school groups had gathered to have photos taken in front of the Capitol. Sizing up the demonstration, their teachers began leading them in a rendition of "God Bless America," which threatened to drown out the press conference. "Some of our people went over and said, 'Show a little respect, do you know who these people are?'" Campbell said. "And these kids did stop singing, and many even listened to what was being said."

Campell described what transpired next—a planned act of

civil disobedience by herself, Wing, Lessin, and McGrath—as happening in slow motion. They walked up the Capitol steps carrying a banner that read, *"Reclaim the Capitol, Stop the War Now!"* Flanked by the Iraqi family and the group of supporters carrying large portraits of Iraqi people, they approached a "staff only" staircase. "The Capitol police told us we couldn't go in that way," Campbell recalls. "They said, 'If you want to get an appointment, we can help you.' And I said, 'We've had appointments, they're not getting us anywhere, so now we need to go in this way.'" As they were arrested and put in flexcuffs, she looked down at the group below. "They started singing, *'Let there be peace on earth, and let it begin with me,'* from my grandmother's favorite song, which was sung at her funeral," Campbell said. "I thought I was going to lose it. But the policewoman who arrrested me, who was younger than me, was so nervous that she was shaking. So I wound up comforting *her.*"

After being hauled two blocks in a paddy wagon, the group spent most of the day handcuffed to a wall in two separate rooms in Capitol Police Headquarters. "Aside from the handcuffs, it was a bit like a hospital waiting room," Campbell said.

Late that afternoon, the group was informed that they would not be charged with the typical fifty-dollar "post and forfeit" they expected, but were instead being charged with the higher penalty of "unlawful entry," and sent to spend the night in jail. (They would be released that same evening, but required to appear in court two weeks later.) It appeared to be a message to others heeding the call for massive civil disobedience the following week: The price would be higher than expected.

It was a symbolic action, but it was indeed enough to kick off other nonviolent acts of civil disobedience across the country. And the following Monday, Adele Welty, Rita Lasar, and Bob McIlvaine would find themselves doing something they had never imagined doing: choosing to get arrested to stop the war.

Rita Lasar is handcuffed

"It means so much to me that the word gets out, that there are families who are against the war, against what Bush has done, against what the United States has done," McIlvaine said. But it would be the first time since September 11 that he would spend the night away from his wife, Helen, and son, Jeff. "That's one thing I've learned, that no matter how much I want to do something, I still have to think of the family. So I asked my wife, and she said, 'Without question, do it.'"

"I wasn't one-hundred-percent sure we would get arrested, and neither was Rita, because we're old," said Adele Welty. "But I was willing to take that risk if it called attention to the fact that Congress had abdicated its responsibility and just rolled over for the President. I thought if old farts like us can get arrested, it might really draw attention that this was not some hippie thing, this wasn't a bunch of rowdy kids from some campus, that a great many of us were older people, and we were doing this because we believed the war was wrong."

Although those getting arrested had been given nonviolence training the day before, it was still a harrowing experience. "I was a nervous wreck, an emotional basket case," McIlvaine admitted, "because it just brought up the memories of what happened on

September 11. We got to the church, and I must have broken down five different times. I was sitting with a girl I'd never seen in my life, and she showed me some pictures of kids in Iraq, and I broke down. I did some interviews, and every time I'd start talking about how I wanted to get meaning out of this, about why my son died, I would break down. It was an emotional roller coaster. But I was happy to do it."

The group left the church, McIlvaine wearing his son's Princeton cap, and arrived on the west lawn of the Capitol to the sound of policemen on bullhorns announcing that the demonstration was illegal—and that those crossing the police line around the building would be arrested. The demonstrators responded with a series of short speeches via bullhorn, and those self-selected for arrest gathered for their final march. They would advance toward arrest in twos and threes, and Adele, Rita, and Bob would lead the way. Linking arms, they each took a deep breath and stepped forward, experiencing their action, as others had, as occurring in slow motion.

"It was totally surreal," McIlvaine said. "All the people are behind us, and the line of police is in front of us, and the police with horses are behind them. The intimidation was phenomenal."

"They were very tall, and they had helmets on, and I didn't know if they'd hit us with sticks, or gas us, or what," said Welty. "It was a little scary to be right up front and not know what would happen. But I saw Maria Hinojosa running alongside with a CNN camera crew, and I thought, well, they're not going to do anything on camera. It turned out they were actually very nice to us."

"We walked up, and their arms were linked, and they didn't look like they wanted to let us through," McIlvaine explained. "So I just said to the fella to my right, a big guy, 'Just let me through, this is very important to me.' So he just opened up his arms, and we walked though, and they handcuffed us. A young guy put the cuffs on me. I had a sign, *'Not in My Son's Name,'* and I had two pictures of Bobby on it, and I said, 'Do I lose my sign?' and he said, 'Definitely.' I said, 'Would you get the pictures off for me?' because I was handcuffed. And he said, 'Sure,' and he took the pictues off and pulled the staples out, and put them in my pocket."

"As soon as he told me to turn around so that he could put the handcuffs on me," Lasar recalled, "the surreal aspect disappeared, and I became totally engaged in this process of arrest, handcuffing, marching to a bus to be taken to the headquarters, the processing of my personal belongings, the very thorough body search, and then the waiting, interminable waiting, until the end of the day. The loss of the ability to move at will, without permission, to go to the bathroom without permission, to speak to Bob across the room without permission, and all the other losses of freedom, gave me an understanding of what it is like to really be arrested. And a realization of what it must be like for all those not as privileged as me."

Unlike their counterparts days earlier, they were given the "post and forfeit" option and left Capitol Police custody with no misdemeanor on their records. *Washington Post* reporter David Montgomery was among the press waiting to interview them as they exited the jail, and wound up taking the group out to dinner. He was a Princeton University graduate, like McIlvaine's son. Just one more small connection among a series of small connections that day: with each other, with others in the peace movement, with the families in Iraq. They had taken their opposition to the war as far as they could go.

Two days later, the first bomb would drop on Baghdad.

September 11th Families for Peaceful Tomorrows condemns unconditionally the illegal, immoral, and unjustified U.S.-led military action in Iraq. As family members of September 11 victims, we know how it feels to experience "shock and awe," and we do not want other innocent families to suffer the trauma and grief that we have endured. While we also condemn the brutality of Saddam Hussein's regime, it does not justify the brutality, death, and destruction being visited upon Iraq and its citizens by our own government.

—From Peaceful Tomorrows' statement on the Iraq War

Chapter Nineteen

Peaceful Tomorrows' statement on the Iraq war was composed during the final week of nonviolent action in Washington. As President Bush gave Hussein forty-eight hours to leave the country, there was little doubt that military action would occur, regardless of the dictator's decision.

In New York on Wednesday night, March 19, Kelly's kids had come back from Irish step-dance lessons and miraculously wanted to go to bed at the same time. As they were going upstairs, her daughter, the youngest, said, "Mommy, can a bomb from Iraq get into our house?"

"I remember saying to my husband, 'We've got to talk to the kids because they're worried and misinformed,'" Kelly said. "To them, Iraq is New Jersey and is right next door. So we turned them all around and brought them to the living room. For about fifteen minutes we told them that the missiles couldn't reach us, that it was a scary world, and we talked about their fears and corrected their misperceptions. We put them in bed, and then we heard about the bombing. I remember feeling this deep, deep sorrow. I always held out the hope that this wouldn't happen, and I felt, 'Oh my god, we're really doing this.'"

Campbell was flying back home to Oakland from

Washington, DC. "I boarded the plane at 8:00 P.M., the deadline that Bush had set for Hussein. As we rose above the Capitol I turned on the in-seat TV set to watch the events unfold. On MSNBC a reporter I had met in Afghanistan was now reporting live, 'embedded' with a unit in Kuwait. On CNN I watched as activists I had breakfast with were hauled away at an action in front of the White House. And then the bombs started dropping. As I looked around, everyone on the plane was watching, too."

In Anchorage, Alaska Andrew Rice was at the end of a week-long speaking tour on the coldest day of the year. He joined a local peace group in a candlelight vigil when the bombs began to fall. "It was very hard being so far away from my family and my support system," he said. "It was the same on September 11—I was out of town, and for about two hours, I was alone. I could not get people on the phone, and I knew my brother was probably dead. The invasion of Iraq reminded me of that day—the sick feeling of seeing the 'shock and awe' on television reminded me of seeing the towers collapse."

Members of Peaceful Tomorows began to call each other, and shared that feeling of flashback: the fear, the sense of upheaval and uncertainty. They knew what it was like to have airplanes come out of the sky and commit violence, and they remembered what it was like to wonder how many more would come, and where they would impose their terror, and who else would die. They remembered wondering if they, too, might die. And they knew for a fact that these feelings would be multiplying among the civilians of Iraq, half of them under the age of 15.

"I had been the last one to say we're not going to bomb Iraq," Lasar admitted. "I really believed it. I said it in Japan. I said it during a speaking tour in the Midwest, and in Tennessee, to anyone who would listen to me. I said the world's opinion is such that this country couldn't possibly begin to bomb. I think I was more devasted than when they bombed Afghanistan. My world was shattered, I lost all my moorings, I didn't know what would happen to the peace movement, to the country, to the world. If we could really do this, then the whole world is unsafe."

If their losses on September 11 had opened their eyes to the realities of terrorism, the eighteen months since then had opened their minds to a host of other realities: the long-lasting effects of violence and the daily experience of war for so many of the world's people; the complexities of relationships among people and nations; the responsibilities they possessed, as citizens of the world's richest and most powerful nation, to do better than to choose violence, in ever-increasing doses, as an antidote to violence; and the need to understand the so-called "root causes" of terrorism. Like it or not, they could never again close their eyes to those realities.

In New Hampshire, Andrea LeBlanc called her daughter, a new parent, and said she was driving to her house.

"I decided that holding her newborn child was more important than watching the bombing on television," she said. "Maybe it's avoidance, but sometimes it's a struggle to focus on the positive things in life. I know perfectly well that unless you do, you don't have any energy, or anything left to give. One of the things that gives me hope is how courageous it was for both of my kids, on the heels of September 11 and the war, to have children. Here they are, saying 'yes' to life. And that's part of my reason for saying, 'Yes, I have an obligation, I have a responsibility here.'"

Potorti sent out the final copy of the Iraq War statement to the staff just minutes before driving to a vigil at the state capital in Raleigh, North Carolina, a planned gathering triggered by the beginning of military action, whenever it might occur. It was approaching 11 P.M., and the air was thick with the scent of an approaching thunderstorm.

"You knew it was going to rain, and you knew that there was

nothing you could do about it," he said. "And as I read our statement to the people there, it seemed like there was nothing we could do about the war, either. But the fact is, we had already done so much—we got connected with each other, and with people all over the world, and we had done everything we could do to speak out against it. I had to remind myself that this wasn't the end—we were just getting started."

E-MAILS FROM AN IRAQI FRIEND
by Terry Kay Rockefeller

The autumn of 2001 was filled—unfairly, it seemed at the time—with achingly beautiful days of bright sunshine and brilliant blue skies. It was on one of those days, September 28, that I traveled to Ground Zero. What I recall now is that my life had become a series of previously unimaginable activities: collecting Laura's dental records, filing a missing person's report, giving DNA samples, requesting an expedited death certificate. So, I guess that when someone told me that relatives of 9/11 victims were being offered an opportunity to go to the World Trade Center site, I felt that it was yet another of the strange undertakings that were coming to comprise my life. Neither of my parents wanted to make the trip, so I was enormously grateful that my best friend from college was willing to accompany me.

On the ferry boat ride down the Hudson River from the Family Assistance Center at Pier 94, a Navy chaplain who had been assigned to accompany us tried to determine what we were expecting to learn and to prepare us for what we would see and experience. That chaplain was a wonderful companion, but there really was no way to prepare for the maelstrom of emotions I would face.

Thick smoke was rising from the remains of the Twin Towers. A landscape of twisted steel and concrete rubble stretched before us. My friend and I said very little to each other, but I remember clearly the first words I uttered: "Someone wanted to do this." It was a statement, not a question. I was overwhelmed by the intentionality of the violence of September 11. The space that the towers had once occupied seemed filled with the hatred and evil that the hijackers had acted upon. I wanted to ask why they had chosen to give up their lives in order to cause such horror. But the nineteen men, whose malevolent intent I felt so keenly, were nowhere to confront.

Fifteen months later, I found myself in a cavernous space staring once again at masses of twisted steel and shattered concrete. No smoke rose over this scene. I was confronted by a crowd of people, most of them men. They were angry and accusing me and my companions of allowing the deaths of their loved ones.

We were in Baghdad, in the ruins of the al-Amiriya bomb shelter. There, in the early morning hours of February 13, 1991, more that four hundred Iraqi civilians, overwhelmingly women, children, and the elderly, were killed when two U.S. missiles hit the shelter. It was the end of our delegation's first day in Baghdad and I was totally unprepared for the virulence of the recriminations the Iraqis were directing at us.

Our encounter began with a formal recitation of the events of that February 13 from the head of the committee that runs the memorial that was organized at the site. Our government minder translated her speech for us. The first missile tore a gaping hole in the four-foot-thick, steel-reinforced concrete roof of the shelter. The second missile entered through the hole that had been created and then exploded inside the shelter. The force of the explosion hurled people's bodies at such great speeds that their skeletal remains were imbedded in the walls, where they still are today. Raging fire consumed all the oxygen in the space. The temperature rose so high that water pipes in the walls burst and both levels of the shelter became filled with super-heated steam. The conditions under which people perished were horrific and there were so many parallels to the fiery end that I imagined Laura endured that I grew sickened by the description.

Next, individuals came forward to tell their stories. One after another they recounted their losses: a man whose wife, mother, and five children had died; another who, having lost his wife and three younger children, was now raising his oldest son on his own; an old woman whose two daughters and all her grandchildren had lost their lives. The members of Peaceful Tomorrows also spoke of our losses on September 11. Unlike the responses I was used to receiving when I told my story to people in the United States, in Baghdad the people seemed (it's hard to find exactly the right sentiment) unimpressed, inured, all too experienced and knowledgeable. I felt also that they did not understand why we were telling them about the events of September 11, while it was very clear to them that we needed to understand what had happened on February 13. Almost every one of the Iraqis we spoke with was convinced that the attack was carried out by precision-guided missiles intentionally aimed at the shelter. And, they insisted, the American military knew full well, after six weeks of war, that the shelter was being used by civilians.

Just why the al-Amiriya shelter was struck by two missiles has been extensively debated. Nothing I could write would contribute new evidence to the theories that abound. Some argue that the missiles were intended for a nearby Iraqi military-communications facility; others that the U.S. believed Iraqi military personnel were inside the shelter; or, that it was just a horrible accident. I left Baghdad feeling that the most important truth I had learned was that the family members of the al-Amiriya victims we met believed that the U.S. government had knowingly targeted their loved ones. Their level of anger was extreme. There was little we could say or do to respond, so we found ourselves facing one after another of the victims' relatives and simply bearing witness to their suffering.

After perhaps thirty minutes the crowd began to break into smaller groups as the Iraqis brought the Peaceful Tomorrows members into a second room in the shelter where framed photographs of those who had died were on display. The frames were large, perhaps two feet by three feet, and in each were grouped photos of the dead from a different family, often five or more. The mood shifted subtly. Sadness and grief replaced rage. More that one person spoke the phrase I would hear dozens of times during our stay in Iraq: "It is not the American people we hate, it is your government."

Over the next four days we visited many other places in Baghdad and we traveled to Basra and into the countryside along the Shatt Al-Arab River in the south. We went to hospitals, schools, university buildings, mosques, and churches. We spoke with doctors, nurses, teachers, students, government officials, and religious leaders. Each of them, it seemed, had lost a close relative to war. Many asked us, "What will you do to keep your government from coming and killing more of us?"

We hoped that the stories we brought home about the Iraqi people we had met would help build opposition to war in Iraq. And in February, as antiwar protests around the world mounted and politics within the UN Security Council unfolded, I briefly dared to hope that the bombs would not fall again. I had been back in the U.S. for about six weeks when I checked my e-mail one morning and was surprised to receive the following message:

March 2, 2003

Dear Mrs. Rockefeller,

I'm Ahmad, I lost my family in Al-Amriya shelter. I met you at Al-Amriya shelter since three months ago, and took your card, and now I'm in Jordan to send you this e-mail, as I need help from you to support my family in Iraq. Waiting your good reply.

Thanks and Best Regards.

Ahmad

I responded:

March 6, 2003

Dear Ahmad,

I am glad that you were able to send me an e-mail. All of us from Peaceful Tomorrows are following events in Iraq very closely and we are continuing to do all that we can to prevent another war.

I do not know exactly how I can help you and your family. Our group does not have any way to send help to individuals, but I can try to learn about other organizations that do. What do you need? Where is your family? How long will you be in Jordan?

Wishing you and everyone in Iraq the very best,

Terry Rockefeller

Ahmad was not counting on peace:

March 8, 2003

hi miss Terry Kay how are u

i hope u r doing fine

really am so glad to hear from u an am wautng your help

my family was died in iraq i just have to brothers in iraq and they dont have any work there in iraq.

am a driver in jordan iraq way becuse that am coming to jordan every week

and stay from 3to4 days in jordan

and as u know myfamily was died

and am waiting your help really i havr hard time now in iraq and as u know

there is no free life there and the war is coming am not ready to lose all

my family in this war just i need peac that is all what and and all iraqian

ppl

ahmad

am looking to hear from

tahnks again

March 12, 2003

Hello Ahmad,

I too do not want you to lose any more of your family to senseless war. Will your brothers come to Jordan with you? What are your plans?

I do not know how I can help you when I am here in the U.S. Our group Peaceful Tomorrows continues to work to change the U.S. government, so that there will be peace in Iraq. Certainly there are many people throughout the world who are working for the same goal. It is my greatest wish that together we succeed.

Please continue to write and let me know where you are and how you and your brothers are doing.

Your friend,

Terry

April 3, 2003

Hello again Ahmad,

I am worried that I have not received another e-mail from you. I am always watching the television to learn how the people of Iraq, and especially the people in Baghdad, are doing. The war is a very sad thing. I really believe that this is a war that did not have to happen. I want you to write to me as soon as you can. I want to know that you are all right. I need to learn how your family and your neighbors are. I am hoping that I can return to Iraq soon. Then "Inshalla" we will meet again.

Peace in the future,

Terry

My last e-mail, on April 30, 2003, was returned as undeliverable.

I don't know if Ahmad ever believed that I could do anything to help him and his brothers. I hope I didn't disappoint him. When I read and re-read his two e-mails to me, I am always struck by the playful way he opened his second message. I feel that he really was glad to receive my reply. That he would confide, "as u know there is no free life" in Iraq, takes my breath away. Why would he trust me enough to say such a thing—a statement for which he might be killed by the Iraqi regime?

With his trust, Ahmad gave me an extraordinary gift. He rekindled my faith in the power that lies in people from different cultures and lives just making an effort to get to know one another. He helped me believe again in the possibility of a world where people put the injuries they have caused one another behind them and aspire to create peace. It was faith and belief I nearly lost at Ground Zero.

September 11, 2002: Lights commemorate the World Trade Center

Epilogue

As of this writing, there are more than eighty family members (and more than two thousand supporters) in September 11th Families for Peaceful Tomorrows. We treasure each one of them for the unique contribution they bring to the group, and recognize that even though the scope of this book did not allow us to mention everyone, that their presence and growing numbers give us a great deal of hope as we pursue this enterprise.

To even begin to thank everyone who made our journey possible would be folly. Let it be said that we could not have created Peaceful Tomorrows without the guiding hand of established peace and justice groups, including Kathy Kelly and everyone at Voices in the Wilderness; without supporters at foundations and individuals who have made financial donations, large and small; and without the support and good will of countless community groups around the country, and around the world, who gave us the strength to carry on. Your kind words will never be forgotten.

Specific to this book, we thank Frances Anderson for sharing transcripts of early interviews with us made during the Walk for Healing and Peace. In addition to producing the *Steps to Peace* video, she has also produced a one-hour documentary of the January 2002 trip to Afghanistan called *Civilian Casualties* (www.civiliancasualties.com). Thanks to Lenore Yarger, a member of the Catholic Worker House in Silk Hope, North Carolina, who joined the delegation to Iraq and shared written details of the group's itinerary. We thank Robert Greenwald, Danny and Victor Goldberg, and Johnny Temple for their enthusiasm about sharing our story with the rest of the world. And thanks to our friends in the media who have written honestly about our group and our goals—you have made a real difference.

A final note about the proposed Afghan Victims Fund: in July 2002, State Department officials told us that concerns over admitting to civilian casualties and setting a precedent for future assistance overshadowed the benefits to American security. But Vermont Senator Patrick Leahy inserted language into the supplemental appropriations bill for 2002 and the appropriations bill for 2003 calling for "repairing homes of Afghan citizens that were damaged as a result of military operations," and further, that "assistance should be made available to communities and families that were adversely affected by the military operations."

While not specifying compensation, these bills did appropriate funds to assist Afghan victims—but as of this writing, virtually the only assistance to specifically reach Afghans affected by the military campaign has been the small private fund raised by Peaceful Tomorrows and Global Exchange.

The full text of press releases and group statements excerpted in this book, along with information on how to support us or invite us to appear in your community, are available by visiting our website: www.peacefultomorrows.org.

RDV Books is a totally independent publishing company founded in 2002 by Robert Greenwald, Victor Goldberg, and Danny Goldberg for the purpose of making available alternative political, cultural, and social views.

ARTBURN by guerrilla poster artist Robbie Conal
with a foreword by Howard Zinn
$19.95, ISBN 0-9719206-1-3, 80 pages, full-color, oversized paperback

"Robbie Conal's art is outrageous, bold, unsparing, and constitutes a welcome offering to the struggles of Americans against war and injustice."
—Howard Zinn, author of *A People's History of the United States*

ARTBURN is a collection of the best pages from the last five years of Conal's satirical monthly column in the *LA Weekly*, updated with background factoids and secret war stories about his subjects, including the likes (and dislikes) of: Dubya, Dick Cheney, John Ashcroft, Rush Limbaugh, Bill, Hillary, and Monica, among others. Robbie Conal has been hailed by the *Washington Post* as "America's foremost street artist." He creates street posters and caricatures satirizing politicians of both parties, televangelists, and global capitalists. His work has been featured on *CBS This Morning, Charlie Rose,* and in *Time, Newsweek, New York Times, Los Angeles Times,* and many other national publications.

IT'S A FREE COUNTRY
Personal Freedom in America After September 11
Edited by Danny Goldberg, Victor Goldberg, and Robert Greenwald, with a foreword by Cornel West
$19.95, ISBN 0-9719206-0-5, 362 pages, hardcover
The most important book on civil liberties since September 11, 2001

"A terrific collection of personal stories, legal arguments, and historical reminders about civil liberties in our society. We must never forget that we live in our faith and our many beliefs, but we also live under the law—and those legal rights must never be suspended or curtailed."
—Reverend Jesse Jackson

A groundbreaking collection of new pieces examining the effects of President George W. Bush and Attorney General John Ashcroft's legislative assault on civil liberties. Contributors include Michael Moore, Maxine Waters, Steve Earle, Howard Zinn, Tom Hayden, Robert Scheer, cartoonist Matt Groening, Michael Isikoff, Dennis Kucinich, and many more.

These books are available at local bookstores. They can also be purchased with a credit card online through www.akashicbooks.com. To order by mail send a check or money order to:
RDV Books/Akashic Books
PO Box 1456, New York, NY 10009
www.akashicbooks.com
Akashic7@aol.com
(Prices include shipping. Outside the U.S., add $8 to each book ordered.)

David Potorti has served as a journalist and as a television and radio writer and producer. He lives in North Carolina and is one of the founders of September 11th Families for Peaceful Tomorrows.

September 11th Families for Peaceful Tomorrows is a non-profit group of family members of terrorism victims dedicated to finding alternatives to war as a response to their personal and national tragedies. Peaceful Tomorrows represents more than eighty people who lost loved ones in New York City, Washington, DC, and Shanksville, Pennsylvania, as well as more than two thousand supporters.